QG QUICK GUIDE **İSTANBUL**

www.quickguideistanbul.com

First Edition, İstanbul 2009
Copyright © 2009 Şerif Yenen

Contact   : Şerif Yenen
Mobile   : +90 533 591 1303
Web   : www.serifyenen.com
E-mail   : sy@serifyenen.com
Address   : PK 14, Acıbadem 81020 İstanbul-Turkey

ISBN 978-975-94638-8-5

Published by Şerif Yenen
Proofread by Diane Hunter
Design by Cem Günübek
Illustrations by Cemil Cahit Yavuz
Maps by Sinan Torunoğlu
Printed in İstanbul by Şan Ofset

Back Cover: Aerial view of the Historical Peninsula - Old City. Photo by Ali Konyalı

Special Sales :

"İstanbul Quick Guide" is available at special discount for bulk purchases
(100 copies or more) for promotions or premiums. Special editions including
personalized covers, excerpts, and corporate imprints, can be created for
special needs or demands. For more information please contact Şerif Yenen.

Contents

Note on spelling and pronunciation

All the Anatolian proper nouns and place names, either in Turkish or in former Anatolian languages, have been given in their original spelling or familiar Latin forms unless they have synonyms in English. Therefore, if you want to read Turkish words correctly, it is recommended that you take a look at "Useful Turkish" section in Practical Information.

Abbreviations

b.	born
C	century
c.	circa, approximately (with dates)
Ç.	çay (river)
d.	died
E	east
F	French
fl.	flourished
G.	göl (lake)
Gr.	Ancient Greek (language)
Ir.	ırmak (river)
L	Latin (language)
N.	nehir (river)
N	north
NE	northeast
Per.	Persian (language)
r.	reigned
sq.	square
Tr.	Turkish (language)

Preface

For more than 20 years I have shared the natural, cultural and historical riches of İstanbul and Turkey with guests from all over the world. For me, the intercultural dialogue makes tour guiding one of the most satisfying and attractive of professions. I have observed that getting to know a country or a city through a person who lives in that culture, breaths that air, in short, through an insider, is quite a privileged experience.

İstanbul is one of the most unique cities in the world, where one can observe the diverse daily life in a setting of ancient history and natural beauty. The people of İstanbul make up a cultural mosaic of different national, ethnic, cultural and religious origins. You can observe the riches of both Turkey and the world in İstanbul, due to this diversity. International cultural, artistic and sporting events, distinguished hotels and restaurants, nightclubs, conference centers, concerts, theaters and cinemas can suit every visitor's taste from any walk of life.

İstanbul is now ready to welcome a greater number of guests than ever before. I would recommend that guests stay for a period of time that would enable them to experience our vast natural, cultural and historical world heritage. As a tour guide from İstanbul, I wish to share information that will enhance your visit, and I prepared this guidebook to fulfill this wish. I just hope that it serves to help you who are visiting İstanbul now and in the years to come.

Şerif Yenen

Photo Credits

Archaeological Museums of İstanbul (Bekir Köşker) > 3, 5

A Publications (Fatih Cimok) > 114, 315c, 316, 317, 318a-b, 326, 334

Ali Konyalı > 37, 48, 56, 59, 60, 64, 92, 94, 96, 98, 100, 102, 105, 106, 238, 240

dDf > 18, 65, 71, 74, 80, 82, 118, 126, 127, 152a,174 226, 268, 270, 275, 293, 294, 296, 300, 312, 313, 314, 315 b, 319, 322, 328

İlhan Kesken > 299a

İzzet Keribar > 76, 142, 147, 151, 158

İzzet Keribar (Musevi Müzesi) > 120, 121

Julian Segal > 40, 52, 54, 77b, 111, 112, 123, 124, 231, 254, 272

Ministry of Culture & Tourism (Mario Novak) > 28, 31,32, 38, 66, 73, 77a, 78, 84, 85b, 87, 108, 172, 225, 357

Şerif Yenen > 23, 26, 42, 43, 44, 52, 54, 68, 69, 79, 85a, 88, 90, 103b, 113, 170a, 170d, 176, 178, 182, 183, 190a, 190b, 191, 195, 198, 202, 203, 221a, 221b, 221c, 224a, 224b, 230a, 230b, 236, 242, 243, 246a, 249a, 249b, 250, 251, 253a, 255, 259, 260, 266, 311, 315a, 321

Yusuf Tuvi > 156, 177

Acknowledgements

Tha author wishes to thank the following for their support and help.

Cumhur Güven Taşbaşı
dDf
Diane Hunter
Emel Budak
Fatih Cimok
Giovanni Scognamillo
Jana Cook
Joan Meyers
Julian Segal
Mehmet Çatak
Ministry of Culture and Tourism
Murat Yankı
Sinan Torunoğlu
Yusuf Tuvi

EUROPEAN
CAPITAL OF CULTURE
AVRUPA KÜLTÜR BAŞKENTİ

İstanbul: European Capital of Culture 2010

*Together with Peç (Hungary) and Essen (Germany),
İstanbul has been chosen as one of the European Capitals
of Culture for 2010.*

The idea of having a European Capital of Culture was first put forward in 1985 when Melina Mercouri was Greek Minister for Culture. Since then this title has been given to cultural capitals.

What will happen in the year 2010 in İstanbul?

The name of İstanbul will be associated with culture and the arts all over the world. As Turkey moves ahead with the process of its candidacy for the European Union, the projects that will be realized will demonstrate that İstanbul, the symbol of the country, has been interacting with European culture for hundreds of years.

The city's cultural heritage will be managed in a sustainable manner and it will become even more of a magnet than ever.

İstanbul will achieve lasting gains in the fields of urban renewal, urban living and environmental and social development.

New museums will be established to protect and display our cultural assets and historical buildings will be renovated, given new roles and opened to the public.

İstanbullites will embrace new artistic disciplines. Young talented people will have the opportunity to become more closely involved in artistic creativity.

With the renovation that will take place, the administrators and administered will join together, hand in hand, sharing their knowledge and experience, to develop a long-term sustainable model for the future.

www.istanbul2010.org

İstanbul is the largest city in Turkey, and though it is not the capital, it is the leading industrial, commercial and cultural center of the country. The population of the city is estimated to be around 13 million.

The Province of *İstanbul* is bordered on the north by the Black Sea, on the east by Kocaeli (İzmit) Province, on the south and southwest by the Marmara Sea and on the west by Tekirdağ Province. Located in a large agricultural region, *İstanbul* Province produces cotton, fruit, olive oil, silk and tobacco. The city is the chief seaport and commercial and financial center of Turkey. A large share of the trade of Turkey passes through *İstanbul*. Industries in *İstanbul* include shipbuilding, liquor distilling and the manufacture of cement, cigarettes, foodstuffs, glass, leather products and pottery. The city is an important rail center, with several international lines terminating on the European side and a railroad beginning on the Asian side.

The oldest institution of higher education in the city is İstanbul University (1453); other major universities are İstanbul Technical University (1773), Mimar Sinan and Marmara Universities (1883), Yıldız University (1911) and the Bosphorus University, formerly the American College in İstanbul (1863), in which English is still the language of instruction.

İstanbul is the headquarters of the Ecumenical Patriarch of the Greek Orthodox Church and the Archdiocese of the Patriarch of the Armenians in Turkey; the city has 157 Christian churches, 17 synagogues and 10 monasteries. Almost 99% of the population in *İstanbul* is Muslim and the city has approximately 2,000 mosques.

HISTORY OF İSTANBUL

Apart from archaeological facts, according to *Strabo*, İstanbul is thought to have been founded in the 7C BC by colonists from *Megara*, led by Byzas. Popular legend has it that the *Megarians*, before coming here, went to the oracle in *Delphi* and asked his advice about where to make their settlement. The answer was "opposite the city of the blind". When they came to the peninsula of the old city, and after seeing an earlier settlement on the Asian side, they concluded that these people must be blind not to have seen such a beautiful place opposite them. Remembering the words of the *Delphic* oracle, they founded their city, Byzantium, derived from their leader's name "Byzas".

During the 2004 excavations for a 78-kilometer (48 miles) rail and subway network that will ultimately link Europe and Asia via a tunnel under the *Bosphorus*, a port was uncovered in *Yenikapı*. Among the finds of the excavation is an 8000 -year-old late *Neolithic* hut containing stone tools and ceramics the earliest settlement ever located on the city's historic peninsula. This will require that the history books be rewritten.

Neolithic Period Grave, Yenikapı Subway Excavations

Yenikapı Subway Excavations*

During the excavations for a rail and subway network that will link Europe and Asia via a tunnel under the Bosphorus, a port was uncovered in Yenikapı.

The Yenikapı dig is carried out by the Archaeological Museums of İstanbul, and it has drawn academics from around the world. With all the finds in the site, one could say, it is the most phenomenal ancient harbor in the world, and maybe, one of the most active harbors of the Middle Ages.

Obviously, excavations and studies carried out in Yenikapı will revolutionize the knowledge of Byzantine-period ship construction. There is no other place that has so many shipwrecks in context with one another.

Yenikapı's 4th century harbor dates back to Theodosius I, and it was active until around 1200. Because silt from the Lykos River and sand from the Marmara Sea quickly covered over the wrecks, the site's ships, bones and artifacts were so unusually well preserved.

Sediment from the Lykos, which emptied into the port, was also caught by the break-water. But instead of flowing out to sea, the alluvial soil gradually backed up, silting up the harbor. By the 12th century, the port was so shallow it was only used by small fishing boats. Four centuries later, the once-bustling harbor was a memory. It also shows that a major earthquake occurred here, probably around the middle of the 6th century.

In addition to the 32 ships dating from the 7th to the 11th centuries, archaeologists have dug up gold coins, clay amphorae, cosmetics cases, bronze weights, wooden combs and porcelain bowls. They've recovered bones of animals and human skulls. Discovered aboard a ninth-century cargo ship was a basket of 1200-year-old cherries nestled next to the ship's captain's ceramic kitchen utensils.

A little below the ships was found an architectural layer of the middle Neolithic / Chalcolithic period with pottery and finds, including an axe. This suggests the coastline here has moved a number of times.

Many finds are currently on display in the Archaeological Museums of İstanbul. An archaeological park with a ship museum is planned after the excavations are over and the metro station is completed.

---

* *Saudi Aramco World*, January / February 2009, Volume 60.

Over the next thousand years, *Byzantium* became a trade and commerce center. But despite great prosperity, Byzantium never distinguished itself culturally, as did so many contemporary cities in Anatolia.

In 330 AD, *Constantine I* allowed Christianity to be practiced publicly, dedicated *Constantinople* as the capital of the Roman Empire, and rebuilt the city splendidly. *Constantinople* itself was not only the new capital of the Empire but was also the symbol of Christian triumph.

The name *Byzantine*, which is derived from the name of the city of *Byzantium*, was given by 19C historians. The *Byzantines* always called themselves and regarded themselves as *Romans*.

In 395 AD *Theodosius I* divided the Roman Empire into two, Eastern and Western. Culturally, the Western part was Latin and the Eastern part was Hellenic. Soon afterward, in 476 AD, the Western Roman Empire collapsed but the Eastern Empire survived. The Eastern

Shipwreck 6, Yenikapı Subway Excavations

The Fourth Crusade (1202-04 AD)

The Crusaders first attacked the Christian city of Zara in Dalmatia. Then, they sailed on to lay siege to *Constantinople*. The Byzantine capital fell on April 13, 1204; it was looted, particularly for its treasures and relics and made the residence of a Latin emperor, with *Baldwin*, Count of Flanders, as the first incumbent.

The sacking of the wealthy city of *Constantinople* in three days by this fourth crusade was so tragic that a Christian high official declared: *"It would be better to see the royal turban of the Turks in the midst of the city than the Latin miter"*.

Romans were Christians and changed their language from Latin to Greek. In the early *Byzantine* period *Justinian I* reconquered the West.

İstanbul is famous as one of the most frequently besieged cities in the world. Before being conquered by the *Turks*, its assailants included the *Persian Darius* (513 BC), the *Athenian Alcibiades* (408 BC), the *Macedonian Philip II* (339 BC), the *Arabs* (673-78, 717-18 AD), the *Bulgarians* (813, 913 AD) and the armies of the *Fourth Crusade*, which twice succeeded in taking the city (1203, 1204 AD). After being taken by the *Turks* in 1453, *Constantinople* became the capital of the *Ottoman Empire* until 1923, when the newly founded *Turkish Republic* declared Ankara (then Angora) the capital. From 1918 until 1923, Great Britain, France and Italy occupied the city.

Under the *Ottomans*, the city went through several name changes, among them *Konstantiniyye, Polis, Stimpol, Estanbul,* and *İstambol*. The name was officially changed to İstanbul in 1930.

Turks in Constantinople (May 29, 1453)

Turks had already tried to settle down in *Constantinople* four times before *Mehmet II*. After becoming **Sultan**, *Mehmet II* immediately built the *Rumeli Fortress* and restored the *Anadolu Fortress* in order to prevent the passage of any reinforcements through the *Bosphorus*.

Preparations, which took two years, included enhancing the fleet and manufacturing cannons.

In April 1453, an army of 200,000 soldiers and a fleet of 400 ships were ready in front of *Constantinople*. In the meantime, the *Byzantines* blocked the entrance of the *Golden Horn* by stretching chains across it. The walls of *Constantinople* were supported with more soldiers. The main intention of the emperor was, in case of attack, to gain time with an expectation of help from the Christian world.

The siege started on April 6 and continued unexpectedly. *Mehmet II,* to the surprise of the *Byzantines*, took his ships to the *Golden Horn* over a hill near **Tophane** by pulling them with animal and human

power on oily wood pieces. A siege of 53 days ended on May 29, 1453. *Mehmet II* ceremoniously entered the city and this considerable victory gave him the title **Fatih** "conqueror" in the Islamic world.

The tolerance of the *Ottoman Turks* has meant that a majority of religious buildings from the *Byzantine* period still exist, if only as churches converted to mosques. Compared to many other countries where these kinds of buildings were generally destroyed, it should be noted that religious tolerance was not a new tradition in *Anatolian* civilizations.

Mustafa Kemal Atatürk (1881-1938)

*"The centuries rarely produce a genius. Look at this bad
luck of ours that great genius of our era was granted
to the Turkish nation."*

David Lloyd George, Prime Minister of the
United Kingdom, 1922

Mustafa Kemal Atatürk, the founder of the *Turkish Republic* and
its first President, stands as a towering figure of the 20th Century.
He achieved so much in such a short time. He emerged as a military
hero at the *Dardanelles* during the *First World War*, and then became
the savior of the Turkish nation in 1919. Leading a series of impressive
victories against all odds, he led his nation to full independence. Then
he proved himself as a great statesman with the proclamation of the
republic followed by a lot of miraculous reforms in almost every field.

*"This nation has never lived without independence.
We cannot and shall not live without it.
Either independence or death."*

M. Kemal Atatürk

*"Mustafa Kemal Atatürk differed from the dictators of his age in
two significant respects; his foreign policy was based not on expan-
sion but on retraction of frontiers; his home policy on the foundation
of a political system which could survive his own time. It was in this
realistic spirit that he regenerated his country, transforming the old
sprawling Ottoman Empire into a compact new Turkish Republic."*
(*Kinross Lord*, Ataturk: the Rebirth of a Nation)

Thousands of his statues or busts and millions of his photos have
been erected or hung all over the country. His name has been given to
countless institutions, buildings, streets, parks and suchlike.

Foreigners unaware of his accomplishments might think that the
Turks are a bit obsessed with a man now dead for approximately 70
years. No other nation on earth has loved a leader as much as the
Turkish nation loves *Mustafa Kemal Atatürk*.

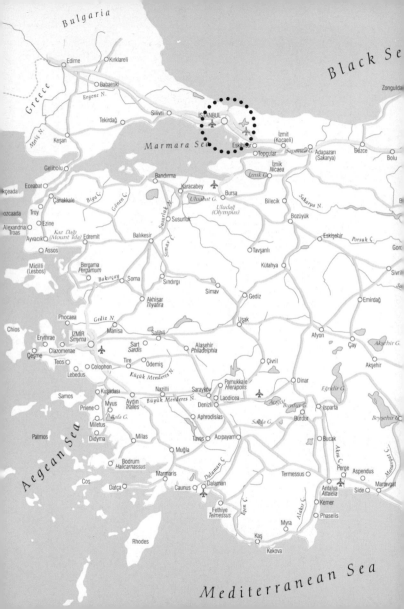

İstanbul

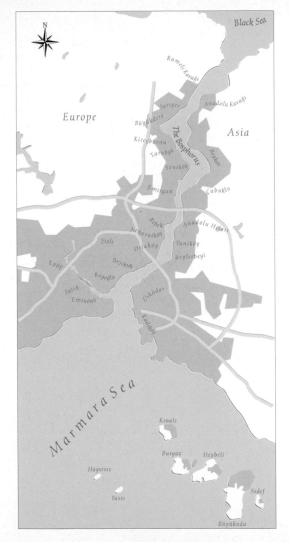

Black Sea

Rumeli Kavağı

Sarıyer
Anadolu Kavağı

Europe
Büyükdere

Kireçburnu
The Bosphorus
Asia

Tarabya

Yeniköy
Beykoz

Emirgan

Çubuklu

Bebek
Anadolu Hisarı

Arnavutköy

Şişli
Ortaköy
Vaniköy

Beşiktaş
Beylerbeyi

Eyüp
Beyoğlu

Fatih
Emirönü
Üsküdar

Kadıköy

Marmara Sea

Kınalı

Burgaz
Heybeli

Hayırsız

Sedef

Yassı

Büyükada

▌ECONOMY

İstanbul Statistics

- İstanbul is among the 20 largest cities of the world, second only to Moscow in Europe.

- 16% of the working population of Turkey is employed in İstanbul.

- Distribution of the economy:
  - > Commerce 34.1%
  - > Industry 23.9%
  - > Construction 71.1%
  - > Transmission & Communications 7.2%

- Share of İstanbul in the Gross National Product is 22%:
  - > 1% in Agriculture
  - > 28% in Industry
  - > 21.2% in Building Construction
  - > 24.6 % in Commerce
  - > 23% in Transmission & Communications

- 46 of the 50 Turkish banks are located in İstanbul.

- 19.5% of the electrical consumption of Turkey is in İstanbul.

- 55% of Turkey's exports (approximately 59.7 billion dollars in 2007) and 58% of Turkey's imports (approximately 99 billion dollars in 2007) occur in İstanbul.

- One of every three Turkish commercial companies is located in İstanbul.

European Union

- The population of the city of İstanbul is greater than 9 of the EU countries. The country of Turkey has the second largest population in Europe.

- Istanbul would have the twentieth largest economy in the EU if Turkey were to become a member.

GEOGRAPHY

The city is situated on both sides of the Bosphorus, the strait that separates Europe from Asia. The European side of the city is divided by the Golden Horn, a tributary that empties into the Bosphorus.

Climate

		JAN	FEB	MAR	APR	MAY	JUN	JUL	AUG	SEP	OCT	NOV	DEC
Average Temp.	°C	6.1	5.9	7.7	12.1	16.7	21.5	23.8	23.5	20.0	15.6	11.2	8.0
	°F	43	42	46	54	62	71	75	74	68	60	52	46
Average Rainfall (kg/m³)		17.3	14.9	13.0	11.3	7.6	6.4	3.9	5.6	7.0	11.3	13.7	16.9

Geology

İstanbul is situated near the North Anatolian fault line, which runs from northern Anatolia to the Marmara Sea. Two tectonic plates, the African and the Eurasian, push against each other here. This fault line has been responsible for several deadly earthquakes in the region throughout history.

ADMINISTRATION

The Metropolitan Municipality of İstanbul consists of many districts or sub-municipalities. The Metropolitan Municipality has a Mayor, and in addition, each district has its own mayor. Elections of mayors are held every five years.

Apart from the mayors, the metropolitan city and each district have a governor. Governors are appointed. A governor is in charge of public safety (police), education, health etc., whereas mayors take care of the environment, water, roads, parks, etc.

RELIGION IN MODERN TURKEY

There are 935 million Moslems in 172 countries of the world today. This is nearly 18% of the world's population. 6% of Moslems live in Turkey.

Although 99% of the Turkish population are Moslem, Turkey is a secular state and people have freedom to choose their religion and beliefs. No one is forced to participate in any religious ceremonies or rites against his will and no one is viewed as being at fault because of his beliefs

Islam

A pious, charismatic man, *Mohammed* was a merchant by trade, who in his youth searched for a purer and more meaningful religion than the polytheistic beliefs that surrounded him.

In his fortieth year he received his first revelation. He was called to be the *Prophet of God* to his people. He began to preach oneness of God and to preach the message entrusted to him—that there is but one God, to whom all humankind must commit themselves. The polytheistic Meccans resented *Mohammed*'s attacks on their gods and finally he emigrated with a few followers to Medina. This migration, which is called the *Hegira (Hicret)*, took place in 622 AD.

In *Medina*, *Mohammed* won acceptance as a leader. Within a few years he had established control of the surrounding region and in 630 he finally conquered *Mecca*. The Kaaba, a shrine that had for some time housed the idols of the pagan Meccans, was rededicated to the worship of **Allah** and it became the object of pilgrimage for all Moslems.

The believers of Islam are called Moslems (Muslims). The Arabic word Islam means the act of committing oneself unreservedly to God and a Moslem is a person who makes this commitment.

HISTORICAL PENINSULA & PERA

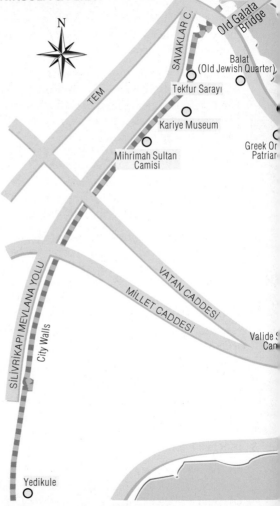

N

TEM

SAVAKLAR C.

Old Galata Bridge

Balat
(Old Jewish Quarter)

Tekfur Sarayı

Kariye Museum

Greek Or
Patriar

Mihrimah Sultan
Camisi

VATAN CADDESİ

MİLLET CADDESİ

SİLİVRİKAPI MEVLANA YOLU

City Walls

Valide S
Can

Yedikule

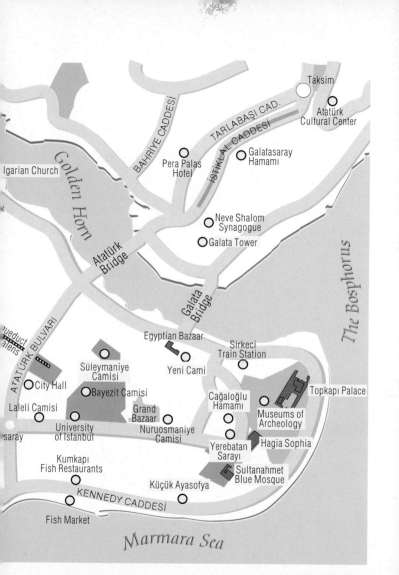

Taksim

Atatürk
Cultural Center

BAHRIYE CADDESİ

TARLABAŞI CAD.

İSTİKLAL CADDESİ

Galatasaray
Hamamı

Pera Palas
Hotel

Igarian Church

Golden Horn

Neve Shalom
Synagogue

Galata Tower

Atatürk
Bridge

The Bosphorus

Galata
Bridge

Aqueduct
atens

ATATÜRK BULVARI

Egyptian Bazaar

Sirkeci
Train Station

Süleymaniye
Camisi

Yeni Cami

City Hall

Bayezit Camisi

Cağaloğlu
Hamamı

Topkapı Palace

Laleli Camisi

Grand
Bazaar

Museums of
Archeology

saray

University
of Istanbul

Nuruosmaniye
Camisi

Yerebatan
Sarayı

Hagia Sophia

Kumkapı
Fish Restaurants

Sultanahmet
Blue Mosque

Küçük Ayasofya

KENNEDY CADDESİ

Fish Market

Marmara Sea

Next page: Hagia Sophia >>

17

Highlights in İstanbul

If you have only one day in İstanbul

HIPPODROME
BLUE MOSQUE
HAGIA SOPHIA
TOPKAPI PALACE
GRAND BAZAAR

SULTANAHMET AREA

Sultanahmet Area was named after *Sultan Ahmet Mosque* (Blue Mosque). Lots of *Ottoman*-period public buildings replaced the earlier *Byzantine* buildings here.

1. Hippodrome
2. German Fountain
3. Egyptian Obelisk
4. Serpentine Column
5. *Constantine* Column
6. Turkish and Islamic Arts Museum
7. Land Registration Office
8. *Marmara University* Administration Building
9. Vocational High School
10. *Sphendone*
11. *Blue Mosque (Sultan Ahmet Camisi)*
12. Tomb of *Sultan Ahmet I*

13. *Haseki Hürrem* Baths
14. *Yeşil Ev* (Green House)
15. Four Seasons Hotel
16. Fountain of *Sultan Ahmet III*
17. Entrance to the *Topkapı Palace*
18. *Hagia Eirene*
19. Archaeological Museums of İstanbul
20. *Hagia Sophia*
21. Basilica Cistern *(Yerebatan Sarayı)*
22. Milion

HIPPODROME

The original *Hippodrome* was built in 203 AD by the Roman Emperor, *Septimus Severus*, when he rebuilt *Byzantium*. *Constantine the Great* reconstructed, enlarged, and adorned it with beautiful works brought from different parts of the Roman Empire when he chose *Byzantium* as his new capital.

Although there is not much left of the original building except the *Egyptian Obelisk, Serpentine*, and *Constantine Columns*, according to the excavations carried out, the *Hippodrome* was 117 m / 384 ft wide and 480 m / 1575 ft long with a capacity of 100,000 spectators. It is said that one quarter of the population could fit into the *Hippodrome* at one time.

During the *Byzantine* period, the *Hagia Sophia* was the religious center, a place that belonged to God; the palace belonged to the emperor; and the *Hippodrome* was the civil center for the people.

Chariots drawn by 2 or 4 horses raced here, representing the four factions among the people. Each faction was represented by a color. Later on these four colors were united as two colors, the Blues and the Greens. The Blues were the upper and middle classes, orthodox in religion and conservative in politics. The Greens were the lower class and radical both in religion and politics. One of these political divisions ended with a revolt that caused the deaths of 30,000 people. This revolt was named after the people's cries of "nika" which means "win" and this *Nika Revolt* took place in 531 AD.

The central axis of the *Hippodrome* was called "spina", and the races took place around it. The races used to start by the order of the emperor and the contestants had to complete seven laps around the spina. The winner was awarded a wreath and gold by the emperor.

The *Hippodrome* was destroyed and plundered in 1204 by the *Crusaders*. During the Turkish period it lost its popularity, especially with the construction of the *Blue Mosque*. The ancient *Hippodrome* changed its name and became **Atmeydanı** *(Horse Square)*, a place where Ottomans trained their horses. The only three remaining monuments from the original building are the *Egyptian Obelisk*, the *Serpentine Column* and the *Constantine Column*.

• The Egyptian Obelisk (Dikilitaş)
Dikilitaş was originally one of the two obelisks which were erected in the name of *Thutmose III* in front of *Amon-Ra*

Temple in *Karnak* in the 15C BC. It is a monolith made of granite and the words on it are in Egyptian hieroglyphs praising *Thutmose III*. The original piece was longer than today's measurement of 19.60 m / 64.30 ft which is thought to be two thirds of the original. It was broken either during shipment or intentionally to make it lighter to transport.

The Roman governor of *Alexandria* sent it to *Theodosius I* in 390 AD. The obelisk is situated on a Byzantine marble base with bas-reliefs that give some details about the emperor from the *Kathisma* and the races of the time.

CONSTANTINOPLE BEFORE TURKS

Great Roman Empire was ruled from here for many centuries.

1. Hippodrome
2. Monuments on the Spina
3. Sphendone
4. Palace of Boukoleon
5. Pharos-Lighthouse
6. Great Palace
7. Marmara Sea
8. Great Palace Grounds
9. Palace Church

Marmara Sea

10. Marmara Sea Walls
11. Baths
12. Hagia Sophia
13. Senate
14. Augustaion
15. Statue of Justinian
16. Public Bath
17. Milion
18. St. John in Diipion
19. St. Euphemia

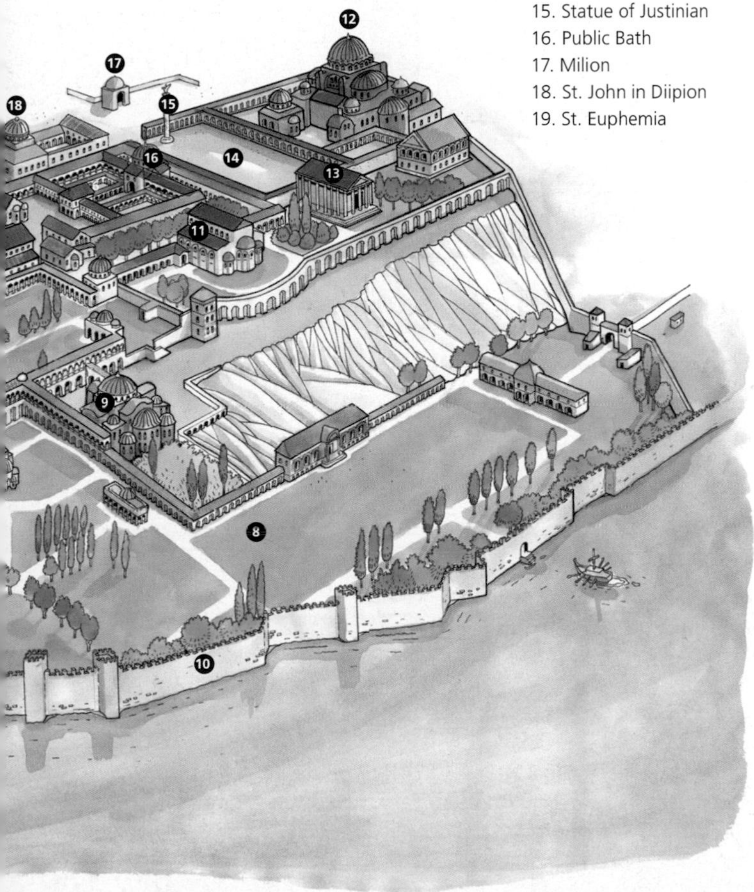

The *Emperor Theodosius I*, depicted on four sides of the obelisk, is watching the erection of it, watching a chariot race,
receiving homage from slaves, and preparing a wreath for the
winner of the race.

• *The Serpentine Column (Burma Sütun)*
After defeating the Persians at the battles of *Salamis* (480 BC)
and *Plataea* (479 BC), the 31 Greek cities, by melting all the
spoils that they obtained, made a huge bronze incense burner
with three entwined serpents to be erected in front of the
Apollo Temple in *Delphi*. Originally it was 8 m / 26.3 ft high,
but today it is only 5.30 m / 17.4 ft.
This column was brought here from *Delphi* by *Constantine I*
in 4C AD. According to records, it stood in its place until the
16C. It is not known what happened to the serpent heads
after the 16C.

• *The Constantine Column (Örme Sütun)*
Unlike the *Egyptian Obelisk*, this is not a monolith but a column built of stones. Who erected it and when it was built are
not known. According to the inscriptions, it was renovated and
restored to have a more beautiful appearance by *Constantine
VII Porphyrogenitus* and his son *Romanus II* in the 10C AD. The
original column would have been from the 4C or 5C AD.

It is 32 m / 105 ft high and after three steps comes the marble
base at the bottom. It is also thought that all the surfaces of
the column were covered with bronze relief pieces that probably were plundered during the 4th *Crusade* in 1204. Today it
is possible to find some of these pieces used in the decoration
of *St. Mark's Square* in *Venice*.

< Serpentine and Constantine Columns in the Hippodrome

BLUE MOSQUE *(SULTAN AHMET CAMİSİ)*

Built by *Sultan Ahmet I* as a part of a large complex, among the Turkish people it is called *Sultan Ahmet Mosque*. However, visitors fascinated with the beautiful blue tiles always remember it as the *Blue Mosque*. The complex consisted of a mosque, tombs, fountains, a health center, kitchens, shops, a bath, rooms, houses and storehouses.

A 19-year-old *Sultan* started digging ceremoniously in the presence of high officials until he was tired. Thus began the

construction in 1609 that continued until it was finished in 1616. An interesting fact about *Sultan Ahmet* is that he ascended to the throne at the age of 14 as the 14th ruler and died only 14 years later. Being close to the *Topkapı Palace*, *Sultan Ahmet Mosque* was regarded as the *Supreme Imperial Mosque* in *İstanbul*. Even at the times when the palace was left and the sultan moved to the *Dolmabahçe Palace*, *Sultan Ahmet Mosque* shared this honor with the Süleymaniye.

The architect was one of the apprentices of *Sinan*, *Sedefkar Mehmet Ağa*. He designed one of the last examples of the classical period's architectural style. The mosque is situated in a wide courtyard that has five gates. There is an inner courtyard next to the mosque with three entrances. The inner courtyard is surrounded by porticos consisting of 26 columns and 30 domes. The *şadırvan* (ablutional fountain) in the middle is symbolic, because the actual ones are outside on the walls of the inner courtyard. There are three entrances to the main building, one from the inner courtyard and one from each side of the building. There are four minarets at the corners of the mosque having three *şerefe*s each. The two minarets at the far corners of the courtyard have two *şerefe*s each. There are six minarets in all, each of which is fluted.

The interior of the mosque is a square with a width of 51.65 m / 170 ft and a length of 53.40 m / 175 ft covered by a dome. The main dome rests on four semi-arches and four pendentives. The diameter of the dome is 22.40 m / 73.5 ft and the height is 43 m / 141 ft. The four piers carrying the dome are called elephant legs as each has a diameter of 5 m / 16.4 ft. There are 260 windows that no longer have the original stained glass. The walls all along the galleries are covered with 21 thousand 17C *İznik* tiles having many flower motifs in a dominant blue color.

Sound & Light Show

On summer evenings, generally beginning at 09:00 P.M., a sound and light show, which is worth seeing, is presented between the *Blue Mosque* and the *Hagia Sophia*. The languages of the show, Turkish, English, French and German, alternate daily.

Interior of the Blue Mosque >

HAGIA SOPHIA *(AYASOFYA)*

The *Hagia Sophia* was probably the largest building on the world's surface, barring the *Egyptian Pyramids*, or the *Great Wall* of China. For many centuries it was the largest church, and today, comparing domes, it is the fourth largest in the world after *St. Paul's* in London, *St. Peter's* in Rome and the *Duomo* in Florence. The great *Ottoman* architect *Sinan*, in his autobiography, says that he devoted his lifetime in the attempt to surpass its technical achievements.

It was dedicated to the *Hagia Sophia* that means the *Divine Wisdom*, an attribute of *Christ*.

Today's *Hagia Sophia* is the third building built in the same place. The first one was a basilica with a wooden roof and was built in 390 AD. This original church *Megale Ecclesia* (Great Church) was burned down in a rumpus in 404. *Theodosius* replaced it with a massive basilica that was burned down in the *Nika Revolt* against *Justinian* in 532. *Justinian* began rebuilding the *Hagia Sophia* in the same year. The architects were two Anatolian geniuses, *Anthemius of Tralles*, an engineer and a mathematician and *Isidorus of Miletus*, an architect. They started collecting materials from all over the empire. In the construction ten thousand workers worked under the supervision of one hundred master builders.

Closed on Mondays

Justinian reopened it in 537, entering the *Hagia Sophia* with the words "Solomon, I have surpassed you!" Because the building is on a fault line in an earthquake zone and the city passed through many riots and fires, the *Hagia Sophia* was destroyed and underwent restorations several times.

Throughout *Byzantine* history, the *Hagia Sophia* played an important role as emperors were crowned and various victories were celebrated in this remarkable building. The *Hagia Sophia* even gave refuge to criminals.

Another major event during the *Byzantine* period was the removal of all religious images from the church in the iconoclastic period. During the *Fourth Crusade* in 1204, the church was pillaged and some disgusting events took place in the *Hagia Sophia*. After conquering *Constantinople* in 1453, *Sultan Mehmet* immediately went to the *Hagia Sophia* and ordered that it be converted into a mosque. This was done by adding Islamic elements, such as minarets, the mihrab, and the minber all of which were appropriately positioned to face toward *Mecca*, 10 degrees south of the main axis of the building.

The architect *Sinan* was also assigned to make some restorations and add Islamic elements to the building. Buttresses were added in the *Ottoman* period. Two huge marble jars were brought from *Pergamum* in the 16C and probably used to keep oil for candles. The eight round wooden plaques at gallery level are fine examples for Islamic calligraphy. The names painted on these plaques are *Allah, Prophet Mohammed*, the first four *Caliphs Ebubekir, Ömer, Osman* and *Ali*, and the two grandsons of *Mohammed, Hasan and Hüseyin*.

In time *Hagia Sophia* became a complex consisting of tombs, a fountain, libraries, etc. It has been thought that when *Turks*

< Hagia Sophia in Moslem period; painting by Fossati

converted the church into a mosque, all the pictures were covered. That is not correct. According to the narration of travelers, some pictures were still standing but the figures' faces were covered.

Hagia Sophia was used as a church for 916 years and as a mosque for 481 years. In 1934, by the order of *Mustafa Kemal Atatürk*, it was made a museum and has since been open to visitors.

• Architecture

The *Hagia Sophia* has a classical basilica plan and the main ground plan of the building is a rectangle, 70 m / 230 ft in width and 75 m / 246 ft in length. The central space of the Hagia Sophia is divided on both sides from the side aisles by four big piers and 107 columns (40 downstairs, 67 upstairs) between them. The space is covered with a huge dome which is 55.60 m / 182 ft high. The dome, due to earthquakes and restorations, is slightly elliptical with a diameter of 31.20 m / 102 ft on one axis and 32.80 m / 107.60 ft on the other.

Main Apse of Hagia Sophia >

• Mosaics

Most of the mosaics are from the times after the iconoclastic period. In the inner narthex above the main entrance, also called the Imperial Gate, there is a 10C mosaic depicting *Jesus* as the omnipotent ruler, seated upon a jeweled throne, dressed as an emperor, and making a gesture of blessing with his right hand. In his left hand he is holding a book inscribed with these words: "Peace unto you; I am the light of the world." On both sides of *Jesus Christ* are two medallions, the *Virgin Mary* on the left and an angel with a staff on the right. *Emperor Leo VI* is depicted kneeling in front of *Jesus*.

On the pendentives are depicted winged angels with covered faces. The ones in the west pendentives are imitations in paint from *Fossati*'s restoration.

Above the main apse is the mosaic depicting the *Virgin Mary* with the *Infant Jesus*.

She is sitting on a bench with her feet resting on a stool. Her right hand is on her son's shoulder and

< Jesus Christ in the Deesis scene, Hagia Sophia
Next page: Hagia Sophia >>

her left upon his knee. Jesus is raising his right hand in blessing and holding a scroll in his left hand.

In the galleries is the 13C mosaic panel of the *Deesis* scene: *Jesus* as the omnipotent ruler flanked by the *Virgin Mary* and *Saint John the Baptist* who are shown interceding with him on behalf of mankind.

Jesus Christ, Constantine IX Monomachus and Empress Zoë

At the far end of the last bay in the south gallery is a mosaic showing *Christ* enthroned with his right hand in the gesture of benediction and the book of *Gospels* in his left·hand. On the left is the figure of the 11C Byzantine *Emperor Constantine IX Monomachus* offering a moneybag and *Empress Zoë* holding a scroll on the right. The emperor's face in the mosaic was changed each time *Zoë* changed her husband. *Constantine IX* was *Zoë*'s third husband.

To the right of the mosaic of *Zoë* there is a 12C mosaic showing the *Virgin Mary* with the *Infant Jesus* flanked by *Emperor John II Comnenus* offering a bag of gold and red-haired *Empress Eirene* holding a scroll. At the extension of the mosaic on the sidewall is the figure of *Prince Alexius*.

At the end of the inner narthex, before going out to the courtyard (today's exit) stands the 10C beautiful mosaic: The *Virgin Mary* with the Infant Jesus in her lap, on one side *Emperor Constantine* offering a small model of the city as he is accepted as the founder, on the other side *Emperor Justinian* offering the model of the *Hagia Sophia* as the emperor who had it built.

Infant Jesus Christ with the Virgin Mary, Constantine the Great (right) and Justinian (left)

43

TOPKAPI PALACE MUSEUM (*TOPKAPI SARAYI MÜZESİ*)

The *Topkapı Sarayı* was the *Ottomans'* second palace in İstanbul. The construction of the *Topkapı Palace*, including the walls, was completed between 1459 and 1478. As different sultans ascended to the throne, each added a new part to the palace. These now represent for us the different architectural tastes and styles of four centuries. The changes were made for reasons of practicality, to commemorate victorious campaigns, or to repair damage caused by earthquakes and fire.

The *Topkapı Palace* was never static but was always in the process of organic development, influenced by the times. The first of these influences was the parallelism between the palace and the empire. As the empire became larger, the palace was likewise enlarged. The second is that as the sultans felt insecure and withdrew themselves behind

Closed on Tuesdays

walls and removed themselves from nature, there was an attempt to bring nature inside the walls in the form of miniatures, tiles and suchlike. If late *Ottoman* period palaces are excluded, only the *Topkapı Palace* survived from the glory days of the great *Ottoman Empire*, which implies that palaces for the *Ottomans* were something different than the ones we know today. There is a kind of humble simplicity and practicality in the *Ottoman* palaces. *The Topkapı Sarayı* was a city-palace with a population of approximately 4,000 people. It covers an area of 70 hectares / 173 acres. It housed all the *Ottoman* sultans from *Sultan Mehmet II* to *Abdülmecit*, for nearly 400 years and 25 *Sultans*. In 1924 it was made into a museum.

The palace was mainly divided into two sections, **Birun** and **Enderun**. There are four consecutive courtyards of the palace;

< Bab-üs Selam (Gate of Salutation), Topkapı Palace

TOPKAPI PALACE MUSEUM

Topkapı Palace, the imperial residence of the *Sultan*, his court and harem, was also the center of the state administration and school *(Enderun)* for state administrators.

A **First Courtyard**

1. *Bab-ı Humayun* (Imperial Gate)
2. Hagia Eirene
3. Imperial Mint
4. Archaeological Museum
5. Tiled Pavilion
6. Ticket Offices
7. *Bab-üs Selam* (Gate of Salutation)

C Third Courtyard

17. Audience Hall
18. Exit from *Harem*
19. Library of *Sultan Ahmet III*
20. *Sultans'* Costumes
21. *İç Hazine* (Treasury)
22. Dormitories
23. Holy Relics
24. Miniatures and *Sultans'* Portraits

D Fourth Courtyard

25. *Revan* Pavilion
26. Circumcision Room
27. *Baghdat* Pavilion
28. *Mustafa Paşa* Pavilion
29. *Mecidiye* Pavilion (*Konyalı* Restaurant and Cafe)

B Second Courtyard

8. *Beşir Ağa* Mosque
9. Privy Stables
10. Entrance to *Harem*
11. *Divan* (Imperial Council Hall)
12. Tower of Justice
13. *Harem*
14. *Dış Hazine* (Weapons and Armory)
15. *Bab-üs Saade* (Gate of Felicity)
16. Kitchens

Next page: Domes of the Harem >>

47

the first two are *Birun*, the outer palace, and the second two are *Enderun*, the inner palace, with the **Harem**.

The first courtyard that was open to the public was entered through the **Bab-ı Humayun** (Imperial Gate). This was the service area of the palace consisting of a hospital (with a capacity of 120 beds), a bakery, an arsenal, the mint, storage places for various things and some dormitories. This courtyard acted something like a city center.

Topkapı Palace, as well as being the imperial residence of the *Sultan*, his court and **Harem**, was also the seat of government for the *Ottoman Empire*, **Divan**. The second courtyard, also called **Divan Meydanı** (Divan Square), which started after the **Bab-üs Selam** (Gate of Salutation), was the seat of the **Divan** (Imperial Council Hall) and open to anyone who had business with the **Divan**. This was the administration center. The **Divan** met four times a week. In the earlier years the sultan would be present at these council meetings, but later on, he would sit behind a latticed grille placed in the wall and listen to the proceedings from there. The Council never knew whether or not the sultan was actually present and listening to them unless he decided to speak. The **Divan** consisted of two rooms, the *Office of the Grand Vizier* and the *Public Records Office*, or *Tower of Justice*.

In addition to the **Divan** there were also the privy stables and kitchens. The kitchens consist of a series of ten large rooms with domes and dome-like chimneys. In these kitchens in those times they cooked for about 4,000 people. The kitchens were used separately for different people, because different dishes for different classes had to be prepared.

In the kitchens today, a collection of Chinese Porcelain which

Religious Holiday Celebrations by the Sultan, Bab-üs Saade

are considered the third most valuable in the world, are on display, together with authentic kitchen utensils and Turkish and Japanese Porcelain.

Just before entering the third courtyard, in front of the third gate, the *Bab-üs Saade* (Gate of Felicity) or the *Akağalar* (White Eunuchs) Gate is the place where the golden throne was placed for all kinds of occasions, such as coronation ceremonies and religious holidays. Payment of the *Yeniçeri* salaries took place there also, as well as the funerals of sultans or handing over of the sancak, the standard or the flag of the *Prophet Mohammed* by the sultan.

The *Enderun*, inner palace, started at the *Bab-üs Saade* and was surrounded by the quarters of the inner palace boys who

were in service to the sultan and the palace. The first building after entering into the third courtyard is *Arz Odası*, the *Audience Hall*. Many important ceremonies also took place there. Foreign ambassadors and results of *Divan* meetings were presented to the sultan in this chamber.

In the middle of the courtyard is the library of *Sultan Ahmet III*. On the right is a section where sultans' costumes are shown. Next to this is the treasury section where many precious objects are displayed. Among these the *Kaşıkçı Diamond* (the Spoonmaker's Diamond) and the *Topkapı Hançeri* (the Topkapı Dagger) are the most precious. The *Kaşıkçı Diamond* is 86 carats, "drop-shaped", faceted and surrounded by 49 large diamonds. The *Topkapı Dagger*, a beautiful dagger ornamented with valuable emerald pieces was to be sent to *Nadir Shah* of Iran as a present, but when it was on the way it was heard that Nadir had been assassinated and so it was taken back to the palace treasury.

From the right-hand corner to the left in this courtyard are the sections of miniatures, calligraphy, portraits of sultans, clocks and holy relics of Islam. The holy relics are personal belongings of the *Prophet Mohammed* (a mantle, sword, seal, tooth, beard and footprints) and *Caliphs*, *Koran* scripts, religious books and framed inscriptions. Relics including a hand, arm and skull bones belonging to *John the Baptist* are also on display in this section.

In the fourth courtyard there are pavilions facing the Marmara Sea and others facing the *Golden Horn*. Among them are the *Baghdad Pavilion* and the *Revan Pavilions* built by *Sultan Murat IV* in the 17C to commemorate his victories in these two cities of Iran.

< Kitchen, Topkapı Palace   *Next page: Audience Hall (Arz Odası), Topkapı Palace >>*

• *The Harem*

The concept of the *Harem* has provoked much speculation. Curiosity about the unknown and inaccessible inspired highly imaginative literature among the people of the western world.

The word *Harem* which in Arabic means "forbidden" refers to the private sector of a Moslem household in which women live and work; the term is also used for women dwelling there. In traditional Moslem society the privacy of the household was universally observed and respectable women did not socialize with men to whom they were not married or related. Because the establishment of a formal *Harem* was an expense beyond the means of the poor, the practice was limited to elite groups, usually in urban settings. Since Islamic law allowed Moslems to have a maximum of four wives, in a *Harem* there would be up to four wives and numerous concubines and servants. Having a harem, in general, was traditionally a mark of wealth and power.

< Harem, Topkapı Palace

Life at the Court

The focal point of the court was the sultan, of course. The *Sultan's* daily life was very simple. In addition to regular daily activities, in order to broaden their perspectives, sultans brought scholars, poets, artists and historians to the palace. Most of the sultans in the *Ottoman Empire* encouraged these skills and developed many skills themselves.

They commissioned new works, manuscripts and bindings, were ardent readers, competent calligraphers, poets, archers, riders, javelin players, hunters, composers, etc. In daily life at the palace, silence was dominant.

The hundreds of people in the palace tried not to meet the sultan unless necessary. In attempting to keep their voices down, it was even said that people of the court sometimes developed a system of body language among themselves.

Topkapı Dagger >

Next page: Ceremonial Hall in the Harem >>

Though the women of the harems might never leave its confines, their influence was frequently of key importance to political and economic affairs of the household, with each woman seeking to promote the interests of her own children. The most famous harems were those of the sultans. The *Harems* of the *Ottoman Turkish* rulers were elaborate structures concealed behind palace walls, in which lived hundreds of women who were married to, related to, or owned by the head of the household.

The idea of the *Harem* came to the *Ottoman* sultans from the *Byzantines*. Turks did not have *Harems* before coming to Anatolia. After the arrival of Turks in İstanbul, sultans built the *Topkapı Palace* step by step. Parallel to it, a harem was also begun. Eventually it became a big complex consisting of a few hundred rooms. The harem was not a prison full of women kept for the sultan's pleasure. It was his family quarters. This was the place where the dynasty lived. Security in the harem was provided by black eunuchs. *Valide Sultan* (Queen Mother) was the head of the harem. She had enormous influence on everything that took place there and frequently on her son too. Young and beautiful girls of the harem were either purchased by the palace or presented to the *Sultan* as gifts from dignitaries or the sultan's family. When these girls entered the *Harem*, they were thoroughly assessed.

Among the girls there were mainly four different classes: *Odalık* (Servant), *Gedikli* (*Sultan*'s personal servants; there were only twelve of them), *İkbal* or *Gözde* (those were *Favorites* who are said to have had affairs with the *Sultan*), *Kadın* or *Haseki Sultan* (wives giving children to the *Sultan*). When the *Haseki Sultan*'s son ascended to the throne, she was promoted to *Valide Sultan*. She was the most important woman. After her, in order of importance came the **Sultan**'s daughters. Then came the first four wives of the sultan who gave birth to children. Their degree of importance was in the order in which their sons were born.

They had conjugal rights and if the **Sultan** did not sleep with them on two consecutive Friday nights, they could consider themselves divorced. They had their own apartments. The *Favorites* also had their own apartments. But others slept in dormitories.

Girls were trained according to their talents in playing a musical instrument, singing, dancing, writing, embroidery and sewing. Many parents longed for their daughters to be chosen for the **Harem**. Women could visit their families or just go for drives in covered carriages from which they could see out behind the veils and curtained windows. They could also organize parties up on the *Bosphorus* or along the *Golden Horn*.

The Chief Black Eunuch had the biggest responsibility and was the only one who knew everything. *Eunuchs*, owing to different methods used for castration, were checked regularly by doctors to make sure they remained eunuchs.

When a **Sultan** died, the new sultan would bring his new harem which meant that the former harem was dispersed. Some were sent to the old palace, some stayed as teachers, or some older ones were pensioned off.

GRAND BAZAAR *(KAPALI ÇARŞI)*

During the *Byzantine* period the area of the *Grand Bazaar* was a trade center. After the *Turks* came to İstanbul, two **bedestens** formed the essence of today's *Grand Bazaar*. They were built by *Sultan Mehmet II* between 1455-1461 in an attempt to enrich the economic life in the city. Later on, as people needed more places for their trade, they also added parts outside these bedestens. In time the *Grand Bazaar* was formed.

Throughout the *Ottoman* period, the bazaar underwent earthquakes and fires and was restored several times. Today, shops selling the same kind of merchandise tend to be congregated together on their own streets or **hans**, as this was originally the *Ottoman* system. In addition to two **bedestens** there are also 13 hans in the *Grand Bazaar*.

With 18 entrances and more than four thousand shops, it is one of the greatest bazaars in the World. The atmosphere of the *Grand Bazaar* is very interesting for tourists and has consequently become a very popular place for foreign visitors.

It is open during working hours on weekdays, closing earlier on Saturdays, while on Sundays and religious holidays it is closed.

< Aerial view of the Grand Bazaar

Next page: Aerial view of the Bosphorus Bridge and the Ortaköy Mosque from the European side >>

If you have a second day in İstanbul

EGYPTIAN - SPICE BAZAAR
BOSPHORUS CRUISE
DOLMABAHÇE PALACE

EGYPTIAN - SPICE BAZAAR (*MISIR ÇARŞISI*)

It was built in 1664 as a part of the *Yeni Cami* complex which is located next to it. *Mısır* in *Turkish* means *Egypt* and it is called the *Egyptian Bazaar* because the shopkeepers used to sell spices and herbs which were brought from or through **Egypt**. During the *Ottoman Period* it was known as a place where shops sold only spices. Today there are only a few spice and herb specialists. The rest sell dried fruit, basketry, jewelry, haberdashery, drapery and suchlike.

The bazaar has an "L" shape with six gates.

Similar to the *Grand Bazaar*, it is open during working hours on weekdays, closing earlier on Saturdays, closed on Sundays and religious holidays.

a. Spice Bazaar

b. Sweets

c. Prayer Beads and Perfume Bottles

< A shop selling spices in the Egyptian Bazaar

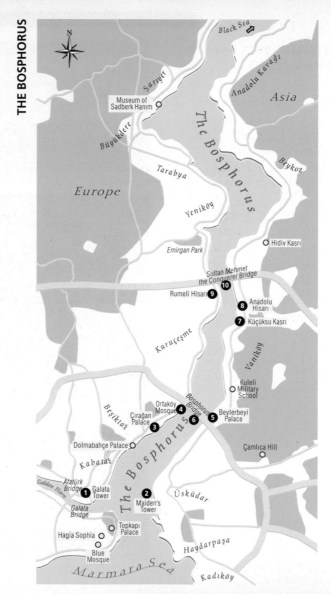

Black Sea

N

Asia

The Bosphorus

Museum of
Sadberk Hanım

Büyükdere

Anadolu Kavağı

Sarıyer

Europe

Tarabya

Beykoz

Yeniköy

Emirgan Park

Hidiv Kasrı

Sultan Mehmet
the Conquerer Bridge

10

Rumeli Hisarı **9**

8 Anadolu
Hisarı

7 Küçüksu Kasrı

Karuçeşme

Vaniköy

Kuleli
Military
School

Bosphorus
Bridge

Ortaköy
Mosque **4**

5 Beylerbeyi
Palace

Beşiktaş

Çırağan
Palace **3**

6

Dolmabahçe Palace

Çamlıca Hill

Kabataş

The Bosphorus

Atatürk
Bridge

Galata
Tower **1**

2
Maiden's
Tower

Üsküdar

Golden Horn

Galata
Bridge

Topkapı
Palace

Hagia Sophia

Haydarpaşa

Blue
Mosque

Marmara Sea

Kadıköy

CRUISE ON THE BOSPHORUS
(*İSTANBUL BOĞAZI* OR *BOĞAZİÇİ*)

The *Bosphorus* is a narrow, navigable strait between Europe and Asia connecting the *Black Sea* (Pontus Euxinus) to the *Marmara Sea* (Propontis).

It is about 31 km / 20 mi long and varies between 1 and 2.5 km / 0.5 and 1.5 mi wide. The narrowest point is 700 m / 2,300 ft between the fortresses of *Rumeli* and *Anadolu*. Swift currents make navigation difficult. The average depth is 50 m / 164 ft. In the *Bosphorus* there are two currents; one on the surface from the *Black Sea* towards the *Marmara Sea* and one below the surface in the opposite direction. The *Black Sea* is 24 cm / 9.5 in higher than the *Marmara* and this causes the current on the surface. The other current is because of the changes of salinity rates in the two seas.

Near the southern end is the *Golden Horn*, the harbor of İstanbul, one of the most commodious natural harbors in the world. In ancient and

You can do the *Bosphorus* tour by hiring a private boat from *Eminönü* between the *Galata* and *Atatürk Bridges*. The other choice will be using the public boat called *"Boğaziçi Özel Gezi"* from *Eminönü* just next to the *Galata Bridge.* It departs at 10:35 AM and stops at the piers of *Beşiktaş, Kanlıca, Yeniköy, Sarıyer* and *Rumeli Kavağı* before it arrives in *Anadolu Kavağı* on the Asian side, close to the *Black Sea*. This ride will take approximately one and a half hours. The same ferry reverses the same route by departing at 3:00 PM from *Rumeli Kavağı.*

Starting from mid-April, an additional ferry will do the same tour by departing at 1:35 PM from *Eminönü*, returning at 5:00 PM from *Rumeli Kavağı.*

medieval times almost all commerce between the *Mediterranean* and *Black Sea* was routed through the strait. It is still an important artery of international trade. An average number of 55 thousand ships pass through the *Bosphorus* annually.

Along both shores are many attractions including ancient ruins, picturesque villages, expensive waterfront homes (yalı houses), and forested areas. Here are a few highlights which you will see from your boat while cruising between the two continents:

❶ *Galata Tower (Galata Kulesi)*

The tower was built by the Genoese colony as part of their town defense fortifications in the 14C. In Genoese sources it was named as *Christea Turris* (Tower of Christ).

It was altered considerably, particularly by the addition of the upper parts under the *Ottomans* during the course of the centuries. It was used at different times as a prison and a watch tower for fires. In 1967, the tower was restored and an elevator was added. The present height of the tower is 63 m / 206 ft. Today two top floors serve as a restaurant with folkloric shows. During the daytime it is open to visitors for panoramic views of the region.

Galata Tower >
Next page: Maiden's Tower with the Old City in the background >>

In the 17C, during the reign of the *Ottoman Sultan Murat IV, Hezarfen Ahmet Çelebi*, a scholar whose first name means "a thousand sciences", managed to fly by wearing rush-work wings, from the top of the *Galata Tower* to *Üsküdar*, an Asian settlement opposite and across the *Bosphorus*. An excited crowd including the sultan watched him achieve this feat. *Sultan Murat* admired Hezarfen but he was also afraid that his unusual ability would win him excessive power. The *Sultan* gave him a purse of gold and declared: "This man is one to be feared. He can do anything he wishes. The presence of such men is not auspicious." *Hezarfen* was then exiled to Algeria where he died broken hearted far from home.

❷ Maiden's Tower (Kız Kulesi)

One of the most distinctive landmarks in İstanbul is the *Kız Kulesi*, originally a 12C *Byzantine* fortress built on a natural rock. The present structure dates from the 18C and was used as an inspection station by the Navy. It has now been restored and made into a cafe and restaurant.

Çırağan Palace

❸ Çırağan Palace (Çırağan Sarayı)

This palace was built by *Abdülaziz I* between 1863 and 1867. This was a period in which all *Ottoman Sultans* used to build their own palaces rather than using those of previous sultans. Unfortunately, because of a fire in 1910 this beautiful palace was just a ruin until very recently when it became one of the most exclusive hotels in İstanbul: *Çırağan Palace Kempinski.*

a. Ortaköy Mosque

❹ *Ortaköy Mosque (Ortaköy Camisi)*

This mosque is also known as *Büyük Mecidiye Camisi* and was built by *Abdülmecit* in 1853. The architect of this baroque style *late-Ottoman* period mosque was *Nikogos Balyan*.

❺ *Beylerbeyi Palace (Beylerbeyi Sarayı)*

The architect *Sarkis Balyan* constructed the *Beylerbeyi Palace* between 1861 and 1865 for *Abdülaziz*. The exterior decoration was adopted from European *Neo-Classicism* but the interior was completed in the traditional *Ottoman Style*. This palace was used both as a summer lodge and as a residence for visiting royalty.

b. Beylerbeyi Palace

Bosphorus Bridge

❻ *Bosphorus Bridge (Boğaz Köprüsü)*

In 1973, on the 50th anniversary of the *Turkish Republic*, a suspension bridge similar to the *British River Severn Bridge* was opened at İstanbul linking the Asian and European shores of the strait.

It is 64 m / 210 ft high with 6 lanes. The total length is 1,560 m / 5,117 ft and the distance between two legs is only 1,074 m / 3,523 ft. The construction took 3 years and the cost was 22 million US Dollars. During its first years pedestrians could walk across the bridge and the elevators inside the legs

were open to the public. However, after many
suicides it is no longer open to pedestrians.

❼ Küçüksu Summer Palace (Küçüksu Kasrı)
A summer palace was built by *Sultan Abdülmecit*
in 1856 upon the ruins of an earlier building.
The style is Western and the architect was
Nikogos Balyan.

Küçüksu Summer Palace

❽ Anatolian Fortress (Anadolu Hisarı)
This fortress was constructed on the Asian shore by *Bayezit I* in
the late 14C, one century before the Turks took Constantinople.

Next page: Rumeli Fortress (Rumeli Hisarı) >>

❾ *Rumeli Fortress (Rumeli Hisarı)*
Sultan Mehmet II made preparations for the siege of *Constantinople*. He decided to build a fortress on the *Bosphorus* opposite the ***Anadolu Hisarı*** in order to cut off the city from its sources of grain on the shores of the Black Sea.

The construction was completed in 1452 in less than four months and it served its purpose well. After the conquest, it lost its military importance.

Today, open-air concerts take place in its theater in summer months.

❿ *Fatih Bridge (Fatih Sultan Mehmet Köprüsü)*
Due to the heavy traffic in İstanbul, another bridge at the narrowest point on the Bosphorus was constructed between the years 1985 and 1988.

This bridge is also 64 m / 210 ft high, but it has 8 lanes. The total length is 1,510 m / 4,953 ft and the distance between the two legs is only 1,090 m / 3,575 ft. The construction was completed by a Japanese company and the cost was 125 million US Dollars.

Yalı Houses

Bosphorus is famous with its yalı houses. These are among the most expensive houses in the world. Prices will range between 20-60 million US Dollars. The word yalı is Greek and it means waterfront. The typical yalı houses on the *Bosphorus* are waterfront wooden houses or mansions. Most of them are from the 19th century. The yalı was originally intended as a summer house. The central area has a wooden dome with spacious bays on three sides; a continuous row of low windows in these bays allow cool breezes to blow through, and offer views of the *Bosphorus* in all directions.

< Fatih Bridge (Fatih Sultan Mehmet Köprüsü) and Yalı Houses

DOLMABAHÇE PALACE (*DOLMABAHÇE SARAYI*)

Towards the end of the *Ottoman Empire*, in the 19C, the Westernization movement was dominant. For the *Ottomans* who lived in İstanbul, "West" was to the north beyond the *Golden Horn*. In the mid-nineteenth century they moved a few kilometers to the north for the *Dolmabahçe Palace*, and this change took the Empire to an entirely different dimension.

"Dolma" is filled or stuffed and *"bahçe"* is garden in Turkish. The site of the *Dolmabahçe Palace* was obtained by filling the small bay on the Bosphorus giving the palace its name.

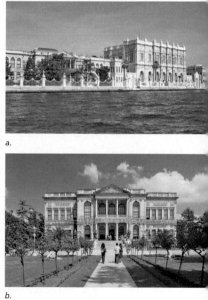

a.

b.

The architect *Garabet Balyan* managed to combine Oriental and Western styles. The lifestyle was Oriental, but the plan was taken from European palaces. He also combined various architectural styles, forming the eclectic style.

It covers an area of 25 hectares / 62 acres. The palace was built by *Sultan Abdülmecit* as the outcome of his Westernzation influences between the years 1844 and 1853. The official opening of the palace was after the *Crimean War*, 1856. *Abdülmecit* lived in his new palace for only 15 years. The palace was used by different sultans

Closed on Mondays and Thursdays

< *Reception Hall with its Chandelier, Dolmabahçe Palace*

until the establishment of the republic. During the republic the palace was used for foreign statesmen and democratic cultural activities. *Mustafa Kemal Atatürk* occupied a room at the palace on his visits to İstanbul and died there in 1938.

The construction of the palace was at a time when the economy of the *Ottoman Empire* was not good at all. This difficult situation was not taken into consideration; all the materials used at the palace were very expensive, of top quality, and brought from different countries. Among the valuable items were *Sévres Vases, Lyon Silk, Baccarat Crystals, English Candelabra, Venetian Glasses, German* and *Czech Bohemian Chandeliers* and *furniture* in the *Rococo Style*.

The palace consists of 285 rooms and 46 halls. There are approximately 600 paintings and very beautiful huge **Hereke** carpets specially woven just for **Dolmabahçe**.

The *Dolmabahçe Palace* is an impressive building facing the sea with very high walls on the side facing inland. The main building is surrounded by magnificent palace gardens. There are nine gates on the inland side, two of which are monumental. On the front facing the sea there are five gates.

The palace was intended to be symmetrical in plan and decoration, not a new idea in architecture; however, with this palace, the focal point was the sea. The building was constructed to be seen from the sea and it is this feature which is new and unique in *Ottoman* architecture.

The reception hall with its five and a half-ton *English Chandelier* and the crystal banisters are of outstanding importance in the palace.

One of the land gates, Dolmabahçe Palace >
Next page: Basilica Cistern (Yerebatan Sarayı) >>

Highlights in İstanbul

If you have more days in İstanbul

BASILICA CISTERN (YEREBATAN SARAYI)

THE TURKISH & ISLAMIC ARTS MUSEUM

ARCHAEOLOGICAL MUSEUMS of İSTANBUL

SÜLEYMANİYE MOSQUE

CHORA MONASTERY (KARİYE MÜZESİ)

BASILICA CISTERN *(YEREBATAN SARAYI)*

Open everyday

İstanbul was one of the most often besieged cities in the world and has always needed permanent water supplies. As a result many underground cisterns were built during the *Byzantine Empire.* Water was brought to these big reservoirs from far away sources through aqueducts. It is still possible to see the remains of a large aqueduct in **Unkapanı**. This is called **Bozdoğan Kemeri** *(Aqueduct of Valens)* and was built in 375 AD by the *Emperor Valens.* Because Turks have always preferred running water, after settling down in the city, they did not use cisterns properly. Most of them were usually converted into either small bazaars or storehouses.

The largest and most ornate of these cisterns is **Yerebatan Sarayı**. In its construction, columns and capitals of earlier temples were used and this provides a very decorative appearance. This is why it is called "saray" which means "palace" in Turkish. **Yerebatan Sarayı** was dug and built probably after 542 by *Emperor Justinian I.* There are 336 columns most of which are topped with *Byzantine Corinthian* capitals. The cistern is 70 m / 230 ft wide and 140 m / 460 ft long. Between 1985-1988, the Municipality of İstanbul cleaned and restored it thoroughly and built a wooden walkway between the columns. In addition to that there are special effects presented by a light and sound show. By looking at the water level marks on the plaster walls which reach the height of the capitals, one can see that the cistern was very full in times gone by.

Two *Medusa* heads were used to form bases for two columns in a far corner of the cistern. The position in which they were placed suggests that the people who put them there were *Christians* and did not want to revere an image of a pagan period. The water inside the underground cistern is collected rain water. The carp in the water are decorative and an incidental protection against pollution. Some think that the *Byzantines* originally also raised fish in the cistern.

< Marble base with Medusa relief, Basilica Cistern (Yerebatan Sarayı)

THE TURKISH & ISLAMIC ARTS MUSEUM (*TÜRK VE İSLAM ESERLERİ MÜZESİ*)

This marvelous museum was the palace of *İbrahim Pasha*, one of the grand viziers of *Sultan Süleyman the Magnificent* in the 16th century. Built of brick and stone, the *İbrahim Pasha Palace* is the only aristocratic residence remaining from the sixteenth century when **Atmeydanı** was surrounded by many such palaces built primarily of wood. It hosted many royal celebrations, such as circumcision ceremonies and marriages of *Ottoman* princes, beginning with the fifteen-day marriage celebration of grand-vizier *İbrahim Pasha* in 1524.

The year in which it was built is a matter of dispute, but it was restored and completed in 1521 and became the palace of *İbrahim Pasha*. After his death, it housed many other viziers and high officials who became members of the Royal family after marrying girls from the Dynasty.

Closed on Mondays

< *Marble Base of the Obelisk in the Hippodrome, and the İbrahim Pasha Palace in the background*

Although three of the original four courtyards have survived to this day, the second courtyard, which houses the museum, is the only one that retains its original design. Many *Sultans* used to come to this second courtyard to watch the festivities and celebrations held next to the palace.

It has housed the *Turkish and Islamic Arts Museum* since 1983. The ticket office, a souvenir shop and an exhibition hall for temporary exhibitions are found on the ground floor.

The next floor has a beautiful courtyard overlooking the ancient *Hippodrome* and the *Sultan Ahmet Mosque*. A traditional style café and an exhibition room on ethnography are also on this floor. The ethnography section contains traditional folk artifacts. The evolution of Turks from the nomadic life in Central Asia to city life in *Anatolia* is seen in this section. Exhibits start with nomadic *"yurt"* and "black tent", and continue with village and city houses, finally reaching the ornate aristocratic houses of İstanbul. Many architectural details and examples of daily life are on display, including carpet and kilim looms, wool paintings, weaving, ornamental samples, regional clothes, handicrafts, nomadic tents, etc.

The next floor is dedicated to the Islamic arts. Among the exhibited works are a select collection of carpets from Turkey and other countries, very fine examples of calligraphy, copies of the *Koran*, imperial edicts, miniature paintings, wooden and stone work, ceramics, and glassware from the Early-Islamic Period.

Carpet collections are among the most important. Beautiful old 12th and 13th century carpets have been preserved using modern techniques and they are shown here to visitors for the first time. Among these rugs are the *Holbein Rugs* and oversize *Uşak Rugs*.

< Detail from a Traditional Embroidered Costume

Next Page: Tuğra (Monogram) of Sultan Süleyman the Magnificent >>

98

• *Holbein Rugs*

These are the 15th and 17th century Turkish rugs with special designs and color combinations. German painter *Hans Holbein the Younger* used these rugs in his works extensively; therefore, they are known as the *Holbein Rugs*.

Hans Holbein the Younger (c. 1497– 1543) was a German artist and printmaker who worked in a Northern Renaissance style. He is best known for his numerous portraits and his woodcut series of the *Dance of Death*, and is widely considered one of the finest portraitists of the Early Modern Period.

Painting by Hans Holbein

Not only *Holbein*, but also Italian painters such as Lotto and Bellini depicted these rugs in their paintings. *Lorenzo Lotto* (c. 1480 – 1556) was an Italian painter, traditionally placed in the Venetian school. He painted mainly altarpieces, religious subjects and portraits. *Giovanni Bellini* (c. 1430 – 1516) was an Italian Renaissance painter, probably the best known of the *Bellini* family of Venetian painters. He is considered to have revolutionized Venetian painting, moving it towards a more sensuous and colorist style. Through the use of clear, slow-drying oil paints, *Giovanni* created deep, rich tints and detailed shadings.

Some features of the *Holbein* rugs have been perpetuated either in the **Bergama** (Pergamum) or **Uşak** (Oushak) rugs.

ARCHAEOLOGICAL MUSEUMS of İSTANBUL (*İSTANBUL ARKEOLOJİ MÜZELERİ*)

The *İstanbul Archaeological Museums* consist of three separate buildings: the *Museum of Archaeology*, the *Museum of Oriental Antiquities* and the *Tile Pavilion*. Thus, its name is always plural.

Osman Hamdi Bey began construction of the Main Building in 1881 and by 1908 the building was as it is today. The architect was *Alexander Vallaury*. The Sarcophagi of Alexander the Great* and *The Mourning Women*, both of which are housed inside the Museum, were the inspiration for the façade. This building is one of the prominent structures built in the neoclassical style in İstanbul.

Osman Hamdi Bey commissioned the *Museum of Oriental Antiquities* as a *Fine Arts School* in 1883. Then it was re-organized as a museum and opened in 1935.

Closed on Mondays

< Head of Sappho

a. Osman Hamdi Bey   b. Main Building

The *Tile Pavilion* was commissioned by *Mehmed II* in 1472. It is one of the oldest structures in İstanbul, featuring *Ottoman* civil architecture. The Pavilion was used as the *Imperial Museum* between 1875 and 1891. It was opened to the public in 1953 as a museum of Turkish and Islamic art, and was later incorporated into the *İstanbul Archaeological Museums*.

Osman Hamdi Bey (1842-1910) was a prominent and pioneering Turkish painter. He was also an accomplished archaeologist, and is considered the pioneer of the museum curator's profession in Turkey. He was the founder of İstanbul *Archaeology Museum* and of *İstanbul Academy of Fine Arts* **(Sanayi-i Nefise Mektebi)**, known today as the *Mimar Sinan University of Fine Arts*.

Osman Hamdi was born into a family of the ruling class of the *Ottoman Empire*. He studied Law, first in İstanbul (1856), and then in Paris (1860). However, he decided to pursue his interest in painting instead, left the law program, and trained under French orientalist painters *Jean-Leon Gerome* and *Gustave Boulanger.* During his nine years in Paris, he showed a keen interest for the artistic events of his day.

< Tile Pavilion

Osman Hamdi married a French woman and had two daughters with her. He returned to İstanbul in 1869.

An important step in his career was his assignment as the director of the *Imperial Museum* **(Müze-i Hümayun)** in 1881. He used his position as museum director and to create nationally sponsored archaeological expeditions.

He conducted the first scientific-based archaeological research done by a Turkish team. His digs included sites as varied as the *Commagene* tomb-sanctuary in **Nemrut Dağı** in southeastern Anatolia, the Hekate sanctuary in Lagina in southwestern Anatolia, and *Sidon* in Lebanon. The sarcophagi he discovered in *Sidon* (including the one known as the *Sarcophagus of Alexander the Great*) are considered among the worldwide jewels of archaeological findings. To lodge these, he started building what is today the *İstanbul Archaeological Museum* in 1881.

When the museum officially opened in 1891 under his directorship, it was the first museum to feature Turkish art. *Osman Hamdi Bey*, founder and director, was also its first curator. The museum was among the 10 most important buildings in the world by the late 19th century. Upon its 100th anniversary, the Museum received the European Council Museum Award, particularly for the renovations made to the lower floor halls in the Main Building and the new displays in the other buildings.

It houses over one million objects: 60,000 archaeological objects, 800,000 coins, 75,000 clay tablets with cuneiform inscriptions, 2,000 Turkish tiles and ceramics, and more than 70,000 books in its library. The exhibits were brought from places extending from the Balkans to Africa, and from Mesopotamia to the Arabic Peninsula or Afganistan. These lands were part of the *Ottoman Empire* at the time.

Detail from a Statue >

Sarcophagi of "Mourning Women" and "Alexander"

The extremely ornate *Alexander Sarcophagus*, once believed to be prepared for *Alexander the Great*, is among the most famous pieces of ancient art in the museum. On the mezzanine level is the exhibit, "İstanbul Through the Ages". Recent finds from the current subway construction are on display in a special exhibition.

The *Siloam (Shiloach)* inscription or *Silwan* inscription is a passage of inscribed text originally found in the *Hezekiah* tunnel, which feeds water from the *Gihon Spring* to the *Pool of Siloam* in East Jerusalem. Discovered in 1838, the inscription records the construction of the tunnel in the 8th century BC. It is among the oldest extant records of its kind written in *Hebrew* using the *Paleo-Hebrew* alphabet. Traditionally identified as a "commemorative inscription", it has also been classified as a votive offering inscription.

Among the collections of the *Museum of Oriental Antiquities*, the most important artifact is the tablet of the *Treaty of Kadesh*. The *Kadesh Peace Treaty*, the first recorded international treaty in the world between the *Hittite* and *Egyptian Empires, Hattusilis III and Ramses II*, in 1284 BC, is another favorite of visitors. Across from the *Museum of Archaeology* is the *Tile Pavilion*, a wonderful pavilion of turquoise ceramic tiles. The building was originally built as a pavilion, and now houses *Turkish Ceramics*.

Other prominent artifacts exhibited in the museum include:

- The *Sarcophagus* of the *Mourning Women*, found in *Sidon*.
- The *Lycian* tomb, a monumental tomb.
- Statues from ancient times until the end of the *Roman* era, from *Aphrodisias, Ephesus* and *Miletus*.
- Parts of statues from the *Temple of Zeus* found at *Pergamum* **(Bergama)**.
- A statue of a lion from the *Mausoleum of Mausolos*.
- A snake's head from the *Serpentine Column* erected in the *Hippodrome*.
- The *Mother-Goddess Cybele* and votive stelai.
- Busts of *Alexander the Great* and *Zeus*.
- Fragments from the temple of *Athena* at *Assos*.
- *The Troy* exhibit.
- 800,000 *Ottoman* coins, seals, decorations and medals.
- The obelisk of the Assyrian king *Adad-Nirari III*.
- Tablet archive containing some 75,000 documents with cuneiform inscriptions.
- Artifacts from the early civilizations of Anatolia, Mesopotamia, Arabia and Egypt.

SÜLEYMANİYE MOSQUE

Süleymaniye, more than a mosque, is an important historical symbol for the Turks. It unites *Sinan* with *Süleyman*, one representing the best of the arts and the other most powerful of political strength.

Like other works of the time, *Süleymaniye* is not only a mosque but a huge complex. It is a work which typifies the *Ottoman Empire* at its peak. Its name, *Süleymaniye*, derives from the builder's name, *Kanuni Sultan Süleyman* (Lawgiver), *Sultan Süleyman I the Magnificent*. The architect was the greatest of *Ottoman* architects, the incomparable *Sinan*.

The *Süleymaniye Mosque* was built between 1550-1557. A spacious courtyard surrounds the mosque. Similar to the *Sultan Ahmet Mosque*, there is another inner courtyard surrounded by porticos with 28 domes supported by 24 columns. This courtyard is a little smaller than the main building. In the middle is located a *şadırvan*. In the four corners of the inner courtyard stand four minarets having a total of ten *şerefes*. The interior of the mosque is rectangular in plan, 61m /200 ft in width and 70 m / 230 ft in length. The main section is covered by a huge dome with a diameter of 27.5 m / 90 ft and a height of 47 m / 154 ft. The dome is held by four piers and supported by two semi-domes in the E and W. The transition to the main dome is provided by pendentives.

The acoustics are among the distinctive features of the building, and were achieved by placing 64 pots in different places in the walls and the floor. Except for those above the *mihrab*, the stained glass is not original. When the mosque was built there were 4,000 oil candles, the smoke from which could have endangered the paintings on the walls. The architect

< *Süleymaniye Mosque viewed from the Golden Horn*

avoided this, however, by creating a system for the circulation of air inside the building. *Sultan Süleyman* and *Sinan* are buried in their tombs in the *Süleymaniye Complex*.

Sinan (c.1491-1588)

He was born in the village of *Ağırnas* in *Kayseri* probably of a *Christian* family. At the age of about twenty, he was drafted for the service of the sultan. After being educated in the palace school, he joined some of *Sultan Süleyman*'s campaigns. His promotion in the *Ottoman* army was parallel to his success in architecture and carpentry. At the age of 48, he was appointed *Mimarbaşı, Chief of the Imperial Architects*, a post he held for half a century during the reign of three different sultans; *Süleyman I, Selim II and Murat III*.

His creativity was born of sensitivity to the cultural heritage and his power of identifying its dynamic points and taking them to their ultimate conclusion. He was not just an architect but an equally accomplished engineer, urban planner and administrator. In his time, *İstanbul* was one of the world's largest cities with all the complex problems of a large urban population. When *Sinan* built, he took into consideration each structure's relationship with its environment and also estimated conceivable future difficulties that might arise.

What were his visual sources? *Selçuk* architecture, churches carved in solid rock in *Cappadocia*, domed churches of *Byzantium* and being well traveled, his accumulated observations. He was constantly driven by the desire to learn to renew himself, to establish links with the past, present and future and to formulate reliable principles. *Sinan* retained this characteristic to the end of his life.

The total number of his works was 477 consisting of mosques, *mescit*s, *medrese*s, tombs, public kitchens, hospitals, aqueducts, palaces, storehouses, hamams and bridges. As an architect who built so many works, *Sinan* never repeated himself, an important feature, and for him, a remarkable achievement. A major aspect of his talent was the ability to transfer any possible architectural problems into esthetic accomplishments.

Interior of the Süleymaniye Mosque >

CHORA MONASTERY - (KARİYE MÜZESİ)

Kariye Museum was originally the center of a *Byzantine* monastery complex. Only the church section, which was dedicated to *Jesus Christ the Savior*, has survived. After the arrival of the Turks in *İstanbul*, this building, like the *Hagia Sophia*, was converted into a mosque. In 1948 it was made a museum leaving no Islamic element in the building except the 19C minaret outside in the corner.

(Closed on Wednesday)
Bus #90 from Eminönü to Edirnekapı
212 - 523 3009

"Kariye" is the Turkish adaptation of an ancient *Greek* word *"Chora"* which refers to the countryside. Considering the perimeter of the walls of *Constantine* (4C AD) the building was located outside of the city. If this theory were correct *Chora Monastery* would be from the 4C. Unfortunately, records do not prove the existence of *Chora Monastery* before the 8C. *Chora* went through many restorations, the last most significant instigated by *Theodorus Metochitus*, prime minister and first lord of the treasury, at the beginning of the 14C. The three most important features of the church -- mosaics, frescoes, and the funerary chapel (Paracclesion) -- are from that period. *Theodorus Metochitus* built the *Paracclesion* for himself and he was buried at the entrance of the church; his grave bears a marble stone. The art of painting in frescoes and mosaics indicated a new *Byzantine* art movement which was parallel to the *Italian Renaissance* started by *Giotto* (1266-1337).

The building consists of the nave, the inner narthex, outer narthex and the paracclesion. The domes of the inner narthex and the paracclesion are lower than the main dome and are only seen from the rear of the church. The drum is supported on four huge pilasters in the corners and four great arches spring from these. The transition is supplied by pendentives. The drum has 16 flutes, each pierced by a window. Entrance to the nave is through both inner and outer narthexes. The niches in the paracclesion were built to keep sarcophagi, as this section was the funerary chapel.

Jesus Christ, Outer Narthex

The mosaics depict the lives of *Jesus Christ* and the *Virgin Mary*. Background elements and architectural motifs are highlighted to give depth. The scenes are realistic, as if they were taken from real life, with figures correctly proportioned. *Jesus* has a humanitarian look upon his face.

The mosaics can be divided into 7 sections: the nave panels, the six large dedicatory panels in the inner and outer narthexes, the ancestry of Jesus in the two domes of the inner narthex, the life of the *Virgin Mary* in the first three bays of the inner narthex, the infancy of Jesus in the lunettes of the outer narthex, the ministry of Jesus on the vaults of the outer narthex and the fourth bay of the inner narthex, and finally, the portraits of the saints on the arches and pilasters of the inner narthex.

Next page: Mosaics, Chora Monastery >>

Kariye Museum Mosaics

Mosaics of major importance are as follows:

The Nave

(1) Koimesis, the Dormition of the Virgin, her last sleep before ascending into Heaven. Jesus is holding an infant, symbol of Mary's soul. (2) Jesus Christ, (3) The Virgin Mary.

The Inner Narthex

(4) The Enthroned Christ with the Donor, Theodorus Metochitus offering a model of his church, (5) St. Peter, (6) St. Paul, (7) Deesis, Christ and the Virgin Mary (without St. John the Baptist) with two donors below, (8) The genealogy of Christ, (9) Religious and noble ancestors of Christ. The mosaics in the first three bays of the inner narthex give an account of the Virgin's birth and life. Some of them are as follows: (10) Rejection of Joachim's offerings, (11) Annunciation of St. Anne, the angel of the Lord announcing to Anne that her prayer for a child has been heard, (12) Meeting of Joachim and Anne, (13) Birth of the Blessed Virgin, (14) First seven steps of the Virgin, (15) The Virgin caressed by her parents, (16) The Virgin blessed by the priests, (17) Presentation of the Virgin in the Temple, (18) The Virgin receiving bread from an Angel, (19) The Virgin receiving the skein of purple wool when the priests decided to have the attendant maidens weave a veil for the Temple, (20) Zacharias praying; when it was time for the Virgin to marry, High Priest Zacharias called all the widowers together and placed their rods on the altar, praying for a sign showing to whom she should be given, (21) The Virgin entrusted to Joseph, (22) Joseph taking the Virgin to his house, (23) Annunciation to the Virgin at the well, (24) Joseph leaving the Virgin; Joseph had to leave for six months on business and when he returned, the Virgin was pregnant, and he became angry. Here it continues not chronologically: (42-44) Miracles.

The Outer Narthex

(25) Joseph's dream and Journey to Bethlehem, (26) Enrollment for taxation, (27) Nativity; birth of Christ, (28) Journey of the Magi, (29) Inquiry of Herod, (30) Flight into Egypt, (31-32) Massacres ordered by Herod, (33) Mothers mourning for their children, (34) Flight of Elizabeth, mother of St. John the Baptist, (35) Joseph dreaming; return of the holy family from Egypt to Nazareth, (36) Christ taken to Jerusalem for the Passover, (37) St. John the Baptist bearing witness to Christ, (38) Miracle, (39-41) Miracles. (45) Jesus Christ, (46) The Virgin and Angels praying.

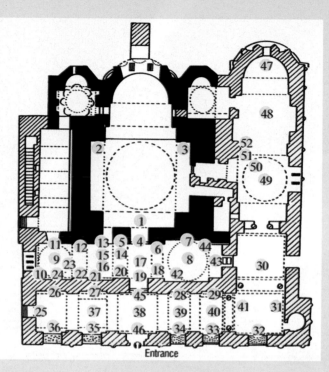

Paracclesion

The pictures here are frescoes. This chapel was designed to be a burial place. Among the major frescoes in the paracclesion are as follows: **(47)** Anastasis, the Resurrection. Christ, who had just broken down the gates of Hell, is standing in the middle and trying to pull Adam and the Eve out of their tombs. Behind Adam stand St. John the Baptist, David and Solomon. Others are righteous kings. **(48)** The Second coming of Christ, the last judgment. Jesus is enthroned and at his side are the Virgin Mary and St. John the Baptist (this trio is also called the Deesis), **(49)** The Virgin and Child, **(50)** Heavenly Court of Angels, **(51-52)** Moses.

Next page: İstanbul Modern Museum >>

Highlights in İstanbul

Places of special interest

JEWISH MUSEUM

KÜÇÜK AYASOFYA (CHURCH OF THE SAINTS SERGIUS AND BACCHUS)

İSTANBUL MODERN MUSEUM

PERA MUSEUM

SABANCI MUSEUM

SADBERK HANIM MUSEUM

MARITIME MUSEUM

FLORENCE NIGHTINGALE MUSEUM

DEPOT MUSEUM

SANTRALİSTANBUL

JEWISH MUSEUM
(MUSEVİ MÜZESİ)

This was originally the *Zülfaris Synagogue* dating back to the 17C. In the early 19C, the building had to be rebuilt on its original foundation. The last wedding took place here in 1983. It has been used as a museum since 2001.

Ceremonial artifacts reflecting the feelings of the *Turkish Jews*, *Torah Scrolls* from various regions in Turkey, an exhibition of photos from their social life and a section on ethnography with objects of birth, circumcision and wedding are all exhibited.

Open 10 AM – 4 PM Monday through Thursday
Open 10 AM – 2 PM on Friday and Sunday
Closed on Saturdays and holidays

Karaköy Meydanı, Perçemli Sk.
(Selanik Pasajı Arkası) Karaköy
212 - 292 6333, 212 - 292 6334
www.muze500.com

121

KÜÇÜK AYASOFYA (CHURCH OF THE SAINTS SERGIUS AND BACCHUS)

This is a prominent building converted into a mosque by the *Ottomans*, originally the *Church of the Saints Sergius* and *Bacchus* which was built by the *Byzantine Emperor Justinian* before 530 AD.

Legend has it that, *Justinian*, before ascending to the throne and during the reign of his uncle *Justin I*, was put in prison for plotting against his uncle. *Roman* soldiers and *Saints Sergius* and *Bacchus*, who are commemorated as martyrs by the Church, appeared to *Justin I* in his dream and witnessed that *Justinian* was innocent. *Justinian* was released afterwards, and showed his gratitude by dedicating a church to these soldier saints right after ascending to the throne. This church was built near the Church of the *Saints Peter* and *Paul*, and the two Churches shared the same *Narthex* and *Court*.

The Church of the *Saints Sergius* and *Bacchus* is also thought to be a palace church for its proximity to the *Great Palace*.

Küçük Ayasofya >

After the *Ottomans* took over from the *Byzantines* in 1453, they did not touch the church until the reign of *Bayezid II.*

Then it was converted into a mosque by *Hüseyin Ağa*, the *Chief Eunuch* from the *Gate of Felicity* at the *Topkapı Palace.*

This was in the first decade of the 16C. In the Islamic period, a portico, a **minaret**, a **mihrab,** a **minber**, a **müezzin**'s lodge, an Islamic cemetery and a medrese have been added to the building. *Hüseyin Ağa*'s grave is in the northern part of the courtyard. Because it resembled the *Hagia Sophia*, Turkish people have named the building ***Küçük Ayasofya Camisi***, which means the *Little Hagia Sophia.*

The building is made of bricks and has an irregular octagonal plan. It is surmounted by a beautiful dome which stands on eight polygonal pillars with pairs of columns in between, both upstairs and downstairs. The transition from the octagon to the circular dome is interesting; the dome is divided into 16 compartments, eight of which are flat and the other eight concave.

The Narthex lies on the West side. Inside the building there is a beautiful two-story colonnade that runs along the sides, and bears an elegant inscription in twelve Greek hexameters dedicated to the *Emperor*, his wife, *Theodora*, and *Saint Sergius*, the patron soldier saint. The lower story has 16 columns, the higher 18. Many of the capitals still bear the monograms of *Justinian* and his wife, Theodora.

Some years ago the edifice, because of heavy damage was added to the UNESCO Watch List of endangered monuments. After an extensive restoration lasting several years and ending

< Küçük Ayasofya

Tuesday through Sunday: 10:00 AM – 6:00 PM
Thursday: 10:00 AM – 8:00 PM
Closed on Mondays
Closed on January 1 and on the
first day of religious holidays

Meclis-i Mebusan Cad.
Liman İşletmeleri Sahası
Antrepo No: 4 Karaköy
212 - 334 7300
www.istanbulmodern.org

İSTANBUL MODERN MUSEUM (*İSTANBUL MODERN*)

İstanbul Modern, the first private museum devoted to modern and contemporary art in Turkey, was founded in 2004 in order to promote wider enjoyment and understanding of modern art among the people. Located on the *Bosphorus*, the museum brings together the cityscape of İstanbul with the arts, which range from painting, sculpture, and photography to video and new media. The museum aims to collect, preserve, and exhibit modern and contemporary art and to provide a venue fostering the integration of the visual arts with the rich cultural heritage of Turkey.

PERA MUSEUM
(PERA MÜZESİ)

The *Pera Museum*, founded in 2005, is the first step of a comprehensive cultural endeavor to provide a cultural service on a variety of levels. It is a distinguished venue and an historical structure, originally constructed in 1893 by the architect *Achille Manoussos* in **Tepebaşı**. Until recently, it was known as the *Bristol Hotel*. Transformed into a fully equipped modern museum, it houses three permanent collections: *Anatolian Weights* and *Measures*, *Kütahya Tiles* and *Ceramics*, *Oriental Paintings*. Temporary exhibitions are worth seeing too.

Tuesday through
Saturday:
10:00 AM – 9:00 PM
Sunday: Noon – 6:00 PM
Closed on Monday

Meşrutiyet Cad. No: 65
Tepebaşı - Beyoğlu
212 - 334 9900
www.peramuzesi.org.tr

128

SABANCI MUSEUM
(SAKIP SABANCI MÜZESİ)

Sabancı Museum is a private museum of fine arts. It has a large collection of calligraphic art, religious and state documents and *Ottoman* period paintings. It was founded by *Sakıp Sabancı* and opened in 2002. In addition to permanent exhibitions, the museum has been hosting very notable temporary exhibitions like *Pablo Picasso*, *Auguste Rodin*, *Genghis Khan* and his *Heirs - The Great Mongolian Empire*, and Islamic arts from the *Louvre Museum*.

Tuesday, Thursday, Friday, Sunday:
10:00 AM – 6:00 PM
Wednesday: 10:00 AM – 10:00 PM
Saturday: 10:00 AM – 7:00 PM
Closed on Mondays
Closed on January 1 and on the
first day of religious holidays

Sakıp Sabancı Cad. No: 22, Emirgan
212 - 277 2200
www.muze.sabanciuniv.edu

131

SADBERK HANIM MUSEUM
(SADBERK HANIM MÜZESİ)

The *Vehbi Koç Foundation Sadberk Hanım Museum* occupies two separate buildings. The original building is a three-story wooden mansion that is believed to have been built in the late 19th century and whose architecture was inspired by European vernacular traditions. The building, constructed of wood and lathe-and-plaster on a masonry foundation, was known as the *Azeryan Yalısı* or *Azeryan Yalı*.

The building was purchased by the *Koç* family in 1950 and was converted into a museum in 1980. The adjacent yalı was bought and added to the museum. This wing is completely constructed of reinforced concrete.

The new section houses the collections of *Anatolian Civilizations* starting with the *Neolithic* and focusing on *Hellenistic, Roman* and *Byzantine* periods. It also has special collections of lamps, jewelry, glass, beads and coins. *Islamic Arts, Ottoman* period artifacts and women's clothes are exhibited in the old section.

Open between 10:00 AM – 5:00 PM daily
Closed on Wednesdays

Büyükdere Piyasa Cad.
No: 27-29, Sarıyer
212 - 242 3813 - 14
www.sadberkhanimmuzesi.org.tr

MARITIME MUSEUM *(DENİZ MÜZESİ)*

The *Maritime Museum* was founded in 1897 at the *Imperial Dockyard*. Originally called the *Naval Museum* and *Library*, a name that was changed to the *Maritime Museum* in 1934, it has the distinction of being Turkey's first military museum.

Original objects that had been removed from İstanbul to various locations in *Anatolia* during the war were put on public exhibition beginning in 1948 in the *Dolmabahçe Mosque* and adjoining buildings. Finally in 1961 the museum was moved to its present location in Beşiktaş next to the monument and tomb of *Grand Admiral Barbaros Hayrettin Pasha.*

In the section known as the *Gallery of Caiques* matchless historic caiques are exhibited.

Instruments used in navigation, ship models and flags, paintings by renowned artists such as *Aivazovsky*, original items from *Atatürk's* yachts *Savarona* and the *Ertuğrul* are all on display here.

Open everyday between 9:00 AM - 12:30 PM and 1:30 PM – 5:00 PM except for Monday, Tuesday, New Year's Day and the first day of religious holidays

Deniz Müzesi
Hayrettin İskelesi Sk.
80690 Beşiktaş
212 - 327 4345
www.dzkk.tsk.mil.tr/muze/English

Opposite page: Grand Admiral Barbaros Hayrettin Pasha

ARIADENVS
BARBARVSS,

(Special permission with copies of
passports is required two or three
days prior to the visit. A contact
number should be provided as well.)

Florence Nightingale Müzesi
1. Ordu Komutanlığı
Selimiye Kışlası,
Harem Ana Kapısı, Üsküdar
216 - 556 8166, Fax: 216 - 310 7929

FLORENCE NIGHTINGALE MUSEUM
(*FLORENCE NIGHTINGALE MÜZESİ*)

In March 1854 Britain, France and Turkey declared war on Russia. The allies defeated the Rus-
sians at the battle of the *Alma* in September but
reports in *The Times* criticised the British medical
facilities for the wounded. In response, *Florence
Nightingale* was appointed to oversee the introduction of female nurses into the military hospitals in Turkey. On
4 November 1854, *Florence Nightingale* arrived at the *Barrack
Hospital* in *Scutari*, a suburb on the Asian side of İstanbul, with
the party of 38 nurses. Initially the doctors did not want the
nurses there and did not ask for their help, but within ten days
fresh casualties arrived from the battle of Inkermann and the
nurses were fully stretched.

The *'Lady-in-Chief'*, as *Florence* was called, wrote home on behalf of the soldiers. She acted as a banker, sending the men's
wages home to their families, and introduced reading rooms
to the hospital. In return she gained the undying respect of the
soldiers. The introduction of female nurses to the military hospitals was an outstanding success.

> "So in that house of misery,
> A lady with a lamp I see
> Pass through the glimmering gloom
> And flit from room to room. "
>
> *(Longfellow, Santa Filomena, 1857)*

The Lady with the Lamp was a pioneer of modern nursing. Her
memory is preserved in İstanbul, Turkey, where a small museum has been founded in a section of the *Barracks* used by
Florence Nightingale during the *Crimean War*.

DEPOT MUSEUM *(DEPO MÜZESİ)*

The historical kitchen buildings *(Matbah-ı Amire)* of the *Dolmabahçe Palace* have been designed as the first *Depot Museum* in Turkey since 2006. Unique examples of many different types of objects like porcelains, crystals, silverware are on display in this *Depot Museum*.

An additional visit to the *Depot Museum* will also complete the tour of the *Dolmabahçe Palace*, as this was a part of the *Dolmabahçe Palace*.

Open Tuesday – Sunday:
9:00 AM - 5:00 PM except
New Year's Day and the first day
of religious holidays

Depo Müzesi
Dolmabahçe Caddesi, Beşiktaş
212 - 227 6671
212 - 236 9000 (ext. 1339)
www.millisaraylar.gov.tr

SANTRALİSTANBUL

The *Silahtarağa Power Plant*, the first power station built in İstanbul in the *Ottoman Period* is being conserved and renovated by *İstanbul Bilgi University* and transformed into a center for culture and arts under the name of santralistanbul. Having supplied the city's electricity from its establishment in 1911 until 1983 from its location at the tip of the *Golden Horn*, the earliest industrial zone of İstanbul, the *Silahtarağa Power Plant* stands out among Turkey's unique national industrial heritage.

This old power station, which covers a very large land, will undoubtedly contribute to İstanbul to take a more effective place in the arts and culture networks worldwide.

It houses an energy museum, lots of cultural activities and workshops for children.

Tuesday through Sunday:
10:00 AM - 8:00 PM
Closed on Monday,
New Year's Day and
the first day of religious holidays

Eski Silahtarağa Elektrik Santralı
Kazım Karabekir Cad.
No: 1, Eyüp
212 - 244 0428
www.santralistanbul.org

141

Unique Experiences

SEMA BY WHIRLING DERVISHES

HAMAM *(TURKISH BATH)*

MEHTER *(MILITARY BAND)*

IMPERIAL BOATS - SULTANS' BOATS

PIERRE LOTI CAFE

WALK THROUGH İSTİKLAL STREET
IN *BEYOĞLU*

SEMA BY WHIRLING DERVISHES

• The Mevlevis

The **Mevlevi** order of whirling dervishes is a mystic group whose members are followers of **Mevlana Celaleddin Rumi**, a great Turkish poet and mystic. The brotherhood is based in **Konya**, where its founder is buried.

Mevlana was never the head of an order, and the brotherhood was not established by himself but by his followers and devoted companions. The order derived its essence, rites, moral code and discipline from the mystical path first shown by **Mevlana**. It was a synthesis of spiritual love attained by a combination of music and whirling which was considered to be the basic requirement for the spiritual devotion.

Mevlana Celaleddin Rumi (1207-1273)

Mevlana was born in 1207 in *Balkh*, Afghanistan. His father, *Bahaeddin Veled*, was a distinguished teacher who, because of his great learning, had been honored with the title of Lord of Scholars. Possibly because of the threat imposed by the approaching Mongolian armies, *Bahaeddin* decided to take his family away from *Balkh*. They went to several places and after staying here and there, *Bahaeddin* felt drawn to *Anatolia* and came to *Karaman* in 1221. There they stayed for 7 years and **Mevlana** was married in 1225.

Alaattin Keykubat, the ruler of **Konya**, implored him to come to **Konya**. *Bahaeddin* finally acceded to the sultan's request in 1228 and he taught in **Konya** until his death in 1231. **Mevlana** took his father's place and quickly established a reputation for scholarship. He had an extensive understanding of all aspects of philosophy and was an avid reader of the works of classical authors.

• His Views

Mevlana was not a man of reason, he was on the contrary a man of love and affection. His aim was unification with God. According to him God could not fit into the universe but fit into the heart. Therefore we have to tend to the heart and not to reason.

> "Come, come again, whoever, whatever you may be, come:
> Heathen, fire-worshipper, sinful of idolatry, come.
> Come even if you have broken your penitence a hundred times,
> Ours is not the portal of despair and misery, come."

Instead of dealing with scholars of the time, **Mevlana** tended towards simple people like *Hüsameddin Çelebi* who was regarded as ignorant by others. According to **Mevlana**, a scholar was like a person carrying a big sack of bread on his shoulder. But, he asked, what was the maximum number of loaves they could eat?

• The Sema

The **Sema** is a 700-year-old ritual or a rite of communal recitation which combines the poetry of **Rumi**, Turkish classical music, chanting from the Koran and the whirling of the dervishes. It was traditionally performed in the semahane. It symbolized the attainment of the various levels of mystical union with God and of absolute perfection through spiritual fervor.

The whirling dervish is the icon of the **Mevlevi** order of **Sufism**, a branch of Islam that is based on the teachings of the mystic poet **Rumi**. In addition to the fasting, praying and study of the Koran that marks the typical practice of Islam, a **Sufi** partakes in *zikir*, or "rememberence", extra practices of which the whirling ritual is the most important.

The sheik is the representative of **Mevlana** on earth. From the sheik's animal skin garment extends an imaginary line across the floor of the chamber which is regarded as the cosmic guide to the ultimate truth. The dervish wears a white coat over a long white skirt, which represents his burial garment. These are covered by a black cloak, which represents his tomb or worldly attachments. The conical brown or white felt hat represents his tombstone. There may be a small difference in the sheik's clothing. The ritual starts with a communal recitation followed by a recital of the flute. Wailing of the flute expresses longing for the ultimate.

They let fall their black cloaks to symbolize their escape from the tomb and readiness for God. Before beginning to whirl, the dervishes bow to the sheik. They bow to one another and move in three rotations to symbolize resurrection and spiritual rebirth. Then they begin to turn slowly. Right arms are above the body palm facing upward whereas left hands face downward. This symbolizes that what they get from God's grace and blessing, they pass on to the world.

The *dervishes* begin to move faster and faster to summon the divine. According to *Mevlana*, with the *Sema*, dervishes can reach out and touch the "ultimate".

Dervishes claim that repeating the Islamic name of God (Allah, Allah, Allah) with every revolution reminds the semazen (whirling dervish) of the *Rumi* tenet: "Wherever you turn is God". It is this that keeps them from getting dizzy, losing their balance or knocking into one another.

It takes at least a year for a dervish to learn how to whirl. The dervishes are everyday people; students, workers, professors, etc. They can have families too.

Galata Mevlevi Music & Sema Ensemble
505 - 678 0618
535 - 210 4565
www.galatamevlevi.com

Turkish Mystic Music & Dance
212 - 458 8834
212 - 458 8835

HAMAM *(TURKISH BATH)*

• *Bath*

The custom of bathing dates from prehistoric ages. In early times, bathing was important not only for cleanliness but also as a social activity and a religious ritual. Public baths achieved their most elaborate form during the *Roman Empire*. Bathrooms were incorporated into the palaces and urban houses of many ancient civilizations. In the *Hittite* capital of *Hattusha* (c.1400 BC), houses contained paved washroom areas with clay tubs, some with built-in seats.

From the 3rd century on, wealthy *Romans* included elaborate baths in their town houses and country villas. These usually consisted of a dressing room, separate rooms for damp and dry heat and warm and cold tubs: *Frigidarium, Tepidarium and Caldarium*. The whole building was heated by a hypocaust-a furnace with flues that channeled hot air through the walls and under the floors. The furnace also heated the boiler that supplied hot water. Reservoirs were supplied by aqueducts.

The public baths (**hamam**) was of special importance in the *Ottoman Empire*. Historians record that the total number of hamams in İstanbul reached 237. Going to a hamam on special occasions (bride, groom, circumcision boy, etc) became a ceremonial ritual and part of the tradition.

The Moslem bathhouse, as an extension of the *Roman* baths, included a dressing room, cold bath and warm bath clustered around a domed, central steam chamber. All areas were heated by a furnace with a system of flues, similar to the *Roman* hypocaust. The **hamam** survived and has developed into the Turkish bath of today.

• *Hamam Experience*

In a *Turkish hamam* there are either two separate sections for each of the sexes or different days and hours allocated to men and women.

When you enter the first section or the changing area of a hamam you begin by taking off your clothes and putting on a *peştemal*, which is a piece of striped cotton cloth. This is wrapped around the midriff and tucked into place. Some people choose to wear their bathing suits underneath or instead of the *peştemal*. A type of wooden clog, called *nalın*, is worn on the feet. They will help you not to slip on the wet marble surface.

Dressed in *peştemal* and clogs, you go to the next room where a *göbek taşı* (navel stone), a marble heated table, is situated in the middle. Marble sinks and taps all around the walls surround the room. Here, you sit next to one of these sinks and start pouring lukewarm water over yourself with a *hamam tası* (bowl). You keep pouring water until your skin softens, meanwhile increasing the temperature of the water as your body gets used to it.

The *hamam* attendant, *tellak*, will take you to the *göbek taşı* when your skin is ready and start rubbing your body with a special glove, kese. Tiny black pieces will get rubbed off your body that most people think is dirt. This is in fact the top layer of dead skin. At this stage a short massage is optional. Next, the *tellak* will give you a soapy rub down and wash you with water in decreasing temperature in order to make your pores close. He will then wrap you in towels.

Now it is time to go back to the lukewarm section to cool your body gradually while you lie down and drink tea in the traditional tiny glasses. Staying too long in the bath or moving to the hot or cold rooms without spending enough time in the lukewarm section is harmful for the body. Otherwise the whole *hamam* experience is something very healthy and cures lots of diseases.

Süleymaniye Hamamı

The Süleymaniye Hamamı was a part of the *Süleymaniye* Complex which was built by *Sultan Süleyman the Magnificent* in 1557. It is a work of the *Great Architect Sinan*.

This is a unisex hamam and they have a pick-up and delivery service

Mimar Sinan Cad. No: 20
Süleymaniye
212 - 519 5569,
212 - 520 3410
www.suleymaniyehamami.com

Çemberlitaş Hamamı

The bath was established by *Nurbanu Sultan*, wife of *Sultan Selim II* and mother of *Sultan Murat III*, to provide income for the Charity Complex in *Üsküdar* built by the architect *Sinan*, in 1584. It was planned as a double bath consisting of two identical, side by side facilities. Part of the dressing room in the women's section was lost when the *Divanyolu Street* was widened in 1868. The side that was cut off was closed with a wall.

Vezirhan Cad. No: 8
Çemberlitaş
212 - 522 7974
212 - 520 1850
www.cemberlitashamami.com.tr

Çinili Hamam

Kösem Sultan had this bath built in 1640 as a part of the mosque complex. It was a small bathhouse built for workers of the complex. The original tiles are gone today.

Murat Reis Mah.
Çavuşdere Cad. Üsküdar

216 - 553 1593 (men)
216 - 334 9710 (women)
www.cinili.com.tr.tc

Sultanahmet Hamamı

The Historical Sultanahmet Hamamı has been renovated from its original 17th century building.

Divanyolu Cad.
Doktor Emin Paşa Sk. No: 10
Sultanahmet
212 - 513 7204
www.sultanahmethamami.com

Gedikpaşa Hamamı

Hamam Cad. No: 65-67
Gedikpaşa
212 - 517 8956
www.gedikpasahamami.com

Kadırga Hamamı

Kadırga, Liman Cad. No: 127
Sultanahmet, Eminönü
212 - 518 1948

Kasımpaşa Büyük Hamamı

Potinciler Sk. No: 22
Kasımpaşa, Beyoğlu
212 - 253 4229

a. Military Band in front of the Dolmabahçe Pala

Mehter (Military Band)

The Turkish Military Band-Mehter is the oldest known military band in the world. Mehter accompanied the Ottoman Army marching into battles for many centuries. With its percussion, it instilled strength, confidence, and courage in the soldiers while intimidating the enemy. The Mehter Band performed in peace times also to help the morale of the people. It was generally a reminder of Ottoman glory, grandeur and magnificence.

The Mehter influenced Poland, Austria, and France to establish military bands. It also inspired European composers, such as Beethoven, Haydn, Bizet and Mozart. These musical pieces were referred to as Alla Turca. Mozart's piano sonata (Turkish March) is a fine example.

b. Aerial view of the Military Museum

Open between 9:00 AM – 5:00 PM
Wednesday through Sunday
Closed on Monday, Tuesday and holidays

Askeri Müze ve Kültür Sitesi Komutanlığı
Harbiye - Şişli
212 - 233 2720

MILITARY MUSEUM *(ASKERİ MÜZE)*

This museum is one of the largest military museums in the world. The building itself was the *Military Academy* in which *Mustafa Kemal* studied during the last years of the *Ottoman Empire*. Wars play a very important role in Turkish history; therefore, with its large collections, it is worth a visit for those who would like to learn more about the history of Turks or those who have an interest in military history.

Another good reason to go to this museum is the regular **Mehter** (military band concerts). They are held indoors or outdoors every afternoon from 3:00 PM to 3:50 PM, except for Mondays and Tuesdays. At the intermission, there are very well done multi-vision shows in both Turkish and English.

In summer months, they perform at the Topkapı Palace at 11:00 A.M. on Wednesdays, and at the Dolmabahce Palace at 10:00 A.M. on Tuesdays.

IMPERIAL BOATS - *SULTANS*' BOATS
(*SULTAN KAYIKLARI*)

There was a hierarchy among boats in *Ottoman* times. The size of the boat, the number of oarsmen, etc. changed according to the rank of the owner.

The boats that sultans used were the largest (30 meters / 98 feet) and the most elegant boats, with 26 oarsmen.

It is claimed that the bird statue, a symbol of the empire, decorating the boat's front, was made of solid gold and the kiosk at the rear (the *Sultan*'s throne) was decorated with precious stones.

The *Sultan*'s outing on the boat was a spectacular event. As the *Sultan* embarked, cannons would be fired from ships

as a procession of smaller boats led the way. People along the seaside bowed to the *Sultan*.

Replicas of these boats have been made and used for special tours on the *Bosphorus* and the *Golden Horn* since 2002.

• Sultan Kayıkları
Kültür Mah. Esra Sk.
Küçük Çamlık Sitesi
B-2 Blok Daire: 3, Etiler
212 - 265 7802
www.sultankayiklari.com

PIERRE LOTI CAFE *(PIYER LOTI KAHVESI)*

The popular cafe overlooking the *Golden Horn* in the **Eyüp** area was the place dedicated to the time that *Pierre Loti* spent in Turkey. He frequently used to go there. The cafe used to have a beautiful view of the *Golden Horn*. Its current view is still beautiful. With the recently built cable car reaching right to the café from the *Golden Horn*, transportation to *Pierre Loti Cafe* has become very easy.

"Pierre Loti" was actually a pseudonym. His real name was *Louis Marie-Julien Viaud* (1850 - 1923). He was a French sailor and writer. His pseudonym has been said to be due to his extreme shyness and reserve in early life, which made his comrades call him after le *Loti*, an Indian flower which loves to blush unseen.

Aziyadé (also known as *Constantinople*) was written by *Pierre Loti* in 1879. It was his first novel and was originally published anonymously. *Aziyadé* is semi-autobiographical, based on a diary Loti kept during a 3 month period as a French Naval officer in *Constantinople* in 1876. It tells the story of the 27-year old *Loti*'s illicit love affair with an 18 year old "Circassian" **harem** girl named *Aziyadé*. The book also describes *Loti*'s "friendship" with a Spanish man servant named Solomon. Some believe *Aziyadé* never existed and the entire work is a cover for a homosexual love story. The book also describes *Loti*'s love affair with Turkish culture which became a central part of his "exotica" persona.

< Pierre Loti Cafe

Beyoğlu is the place where the heart of the city beats for 24 hours. Things you can do in Beyoğlu are a lot:

- Take a nostalgic tram ride
- See shops in İstiklal Street
- See antiques shops in Çukurcuma
- Visit churches or synagogues
- See the Neoclassical and Art Nouveau buildings in İstiklal Street
- Visit cultural centers, bookstores, art galleries or museums
- See the food and fish market near Nevizade
- Eat or drink something together with the locals either at the Asmalımescit, Nevizade or İstiklal Streets
- Visit the francophone pubs, cafés and restaurants playing live French music in Cezayir Street (La Rue Française)

**WALK THROUGH
İSTİKLAL STREET
IN *BEYOĞLU***

Galata
Tower

✿ Neve Shalom
● Synagogue

Galata
Mevlevihanesi ●

● Tünel
(Historic Tunnel)

Nostalgic
Tram Stop

● Tünel Passage

ASMALIMESCIT

Babylon
● Jazz Bar

● Pera Palace Hotel

Swedish Consulate ●

● British Consulate

Russian Consulate ●

● Odakule

● Pera Museum

Dutch Consulate ●
● Muammer Karaca
Theater House

Aznavur Passage ●

St. Anthony of Padua ✝
Catholic Church ●

Yapı ve Kredi Cultural Center ●

Fish Market

Post Office ●

Çiçek Pasajı
(Flower Passage) ●

NEVIZADE
Pubs & Cafes
Restaurants

Galatasaray ●
High School

District
Governor's
Office ●

Cezayir Street
(La Rue Française) ▾

Alkazar
Cinema House ●

● Greek Consulate

Hacı Abdullah
● Restaurant

ÇUKURCUMA
Antiques District

☽ Hüseyin Ağa
Mosque

● AFM Cinema House

● Ak Sanat Cultural Center

Hacı Baba Restaurant ●

✝
Hagia Triada Greek
Orthodox Church

● French Consulate &
Cultural Center

Nostalgic
Tram Stop

TAKSİM
SQUARE

Taksim Republic
Monument

Next page: The Science Center

159

If you have children with you

TOY MUSEUM
(OYUNCAK MÜZESİ)

This is the first and only private
toy museum in Turkey, opened in
2005. Each room resembles a different theater stage. For instance,
when you enter the gallery of
space toys, you encounter shining
stars overhead, whereas miniature train sets are exhibited in a
genuine train compartment. You
have to pass through a submarine
in order to reach the toilets in the
basement. Visitors can relax in
the cafe where antique dolls, doll-
houses, and miniature furniture are
displayed on the walls.

Tuesday through Friday: 9:30 AM – 6 PM
Saturday & Sunday: 9:30 AM – 7 PM
Closed on Monday

Ömerpaşa Cad.
Dr. Zeki Zeren Sk. No: 17
Göztepe
216 - 359 4550, 216 - 359 4551
www.istanbuloyuncakmuzesi.com

MINIATURK

Miniaturk is one of the largest miniature parks in the world today. It has been open to visitors since 2003. Aiming to create a fairy tale atmosphere, the *Miniaturk* project is divided into three main sections, Anatolia, İstanbul and the former *Ottoman* territories. The sections are separated from one another by small landscape designs that ensure continuity by guiding visitors throughout their visit.

Special attention was paid to include every civilization that ruled in and around Anatolia and left its mark. *Miniaturk* traces a 3000-year history from *Antiquity* to *Byzantium*, from *Seljuks* to the *Ottoman Empire* and into the present day.

Kids can feel like *Gulliver* among the small size monuments in this park.

Open everyday 9 AM – 5 PM

İmrahor Caddesi
Borsa Durağı Mevkii
Sütlüce 34445
Beyoğlu
212 - 222 2882
www.miniaturk.com.tr

RAHMİ KOÇ MUSEUM *(RAHMİ KOÇ MÜZESİ)*

The *Rahmi Koç Museum* is the first major museum in Turkey dedicated to the history of Transport, Industry and Communications. Housed in magnificent buildings - themselves prime examples of industrial archaeology - on the shore of the historic *Golden Horn*, the collection contains thousands of items, from gramophone needles to full sized ships and aircraft. The museum educates, informs, and entertains tens of thousands of children each year.

Kids love the hands-on gallery. Where else can you climb all over a vintage car, sit in the cockpit of a real plane and try the controls, or try real-life scientific experiments? And if that is not enough, go there on the weekend and join the special activities.

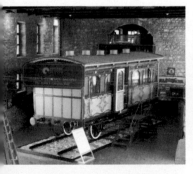 

Tuesday through Friday: 10 AM – 5 PM
Saturday & Sunday: 10 AM – 7 PM
Closed on Monday and holidays

Rahmi Koç Museum
Hasköy Cad. No: 27
34445 Hasköy
212 - 369 6600, 212 - 369 6601
www.rmk-museum.org.tr

RUMELİ FORTRESS

Visiting the *Rumeli Fortress* with kids who are able to run and climb up will be great fun. (See *Rumeli Fortress* in the Bosphorus Tours in the Highlights section)

BASILICA CISTERN (*YEREBATAN*)

This underground building with water and fish is an attraction for children. (See Basilica Cistern in the Highlights section)

ARCHAEOLOGICAL MUSEUMS OF İSTANBUL

The Children's Section of this museum is worth taking your kids to, as it is a good first step in acquainting children with museums and with cultural heritage. (See Archaeological Museums of İstanbul in the Highlights section)

MILITARY BAND (*MEHTER*) CONCERT

(See Unique Experiences section.)

BOĞAZİÇİ ZOO AND BOTANICAL GARDEN

Bosphorus Zoo and *Botanical Garden* is a nice little zoo with 3000 animals of 300 various species and 500 different kinds of botanical plants.

Tuzla Cad, No: 15
41870 Bayramoğlu
Darıca - Gebze
262 - 653 6666
www.bosphoruszoo.com.tr

HORSE CARRIAGE TOUR ON THE PRINCES' ISLANDS

Horse carriages can accomodate four people for a tour of the Islands, *Büyükada* or *Heybeli*. This will be a nice experience with your children.

ŞİŞLİ SCIENCE CENTER (*ŞİŞLİ BELEDİYESİ BİLİM MERKEZİ*)

The Science Center has hands-on experimental and theoretical opportunities for children at various educational levels.

Open everyday: 9 AM – 6 PM Closed on the first day of religious holidays.

Öğretmen Haşim Çeken Cad. Polat Tower yanı, Fulya 212 - 266 0046 www.bilimmerkezi.org.tr

PARTYKIDS PARKORMAN

Büyükdere Cad. Parkorman, Maslak 212 - 276 4060 www.partykids.com.tr

GO FISHING

Children enjoy fishing with their fathers. You will see hundreds of people fishing from the *Galata* or *Atatürk Bridges* on the *Golden Horn* or anywhere on the *Bosphorus*. You can buy fishing line and anything else you need on the spot. You do not need a license for fishing.

THE PLAY BARN

19 Mayıs Cad.
Arkon Residence No: 22
D: 20, Şişli
212 - 217 8797
www.theplaybarn.com.tr

İASK - PONY CLUB (*İSTANBUL ATLI SPOR KULÜBÜ*)

Maslak Üç Yol Mevkii
Binicilik Tesisleri
Maslak
212 - 276 2056
212 - 286 3840
www.istanbulatlisporkulubu.com

Short Escapes
from İstanbul

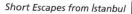

PRINCES' ISLANDS *(ADALAR)*

An archipelago consisting of nine islands is just a few miles from Asian İstanbul in the *Marmara Sea*. It takes less than an hour by ferry from the center of the city. The islands are free of cars and have many beautiful wooden houses. There is a resort atmosphere that offers peace and quiet in a natural environment. Walks or tours with horse-drawn carriages through the streets of the islands, restaurants and cafes are among the simple joys to be found on these peaceful islands.

During the *Byzantine* period, the islands were collectively a religious center with many monasteries. The islands came to be called *Princes' Islands* because those princes who were regarded as pretenders to the throne were sent there in exile. During the *Ottoman* period, the islands were a neglected backwater of little interest. Non-Moslem groups were attracted to the islands. The settlement of a steady Turkish population on the islands came about as late as the end of the 19C.

Ferry Station at Büyükada

All nine islands together form a municipality, the mayor being in *Büyükada*, the largest. *Büyükada* and other large ones, *Heybeli, Burgaz,* and *Kınalı Ada*, have permanent settlements.

Sedef Adası is also recently becoming subject to new settlement. Currently the number of permanent residents on the islands is more than 15,000; however, this number increases more than tenfold during the summer, especially after the school year ends, and summer homes are inhabited.

Büyükada was called *Megalo* in the *Byzantine* period, both names having the same meaning: big. The majority of the population there, at present are Jewish. Because *Kınalı Ada* is closest to İstanbul it was called *Proti* which meant first. *Kınalı Ada* in Turkish means *dyed with henna*. Today, predominantly Armenians live there. *Burgaz* was called *Panormos* in the Byzantine period and is famous as the home of a *Rum* minority and a well known writer of short stories, *Sait Faik Abasıyanık*. *Heybeli* was called *Khalkitis* because of its copper mines. Heybeli is a Turkish name meaning *saddle-bag* and the shape of the island is similar to a *saddle-bag*. The other four islands are of minor importance with no inhabitants. Their names are *Kaşık Adası, Yassı Ada, Sivri Ada* and *Hayırsız Ada (Tavşan Adası)*.

(*Public Boats or Sea Buses from* **Kabataş, Sirkeci** *or* **Bostancı** *are available.* For timetables and lines, you can check www.ido.com.tr)

BURSA

Bursa was the first capital of the *Ottomans* between 1326 and 1364. The city is also known as **Yeşil** (green) **Bursa** because many of its 15C buildings are painted this color. *Bursa* is very rich in thermal springs. Today it is the center of the Turkish silk industry, producing silk not only for fabrics but also for world-famous silk carpets.

Highlights in *Bursa* are the 15C *Green Mosque* and *Green Tomb, Ulucami (Great Mosque of Bursa), Koza Han (Silk Market), Muradiye* and genuine bath houses **(hamams)** with thermal water. Located just next to the city of *Bursa, Uludağ* is one of the most popular skiing centers in Turkey.

Ulucami (Great Mosque of Bursa)

Next page: Koza Han >>

EDİRNE

Very close the *Bulgarian* border, reachable via a very good highway is another Turkish city, called *Edirne*. This was the capital of the *Ottoman Empire* after Bursa and before İstanbul became the capital in 1453. There are lots of beautiful 14 and 15C *Ottoman* buildings, among which are mosques, hospitals, medreses and most importantly the masterpiece of the *Great Architect Sinan*, the *Selimiye* and the complex of *Sultan Bayezid II, Health Museum.*

Meriç Bridge

Oil Wrestling

A very interesting sport from the area of *Edirne* is oil wrestling. It is a tradi-tional sport which goes back to the early times of the *Ottoman Empire*. Wrestlers spread oil all over their body to make wrestling more challenging. Oil wrestling is common in most parts of the country but the most important one is the festival and championship held in *Edirne* annually every June.

< Selimiye Mosque

TROY & GALLIPOLI

Homer's mythological city of *Troy* is just a few hours' drive from İstanbul, a *Bronze Age* settlement with its nine layers. There is so much to see there in addition to what you might imagine seeing.

Once you are there you will also see the battlefields of the *Gallipoli Campaign* of 1915 from the *First World War*. This was an Allied attempt to knock Ottoman Turkey out of *World War I* and reopen a supply route to Russia. The initial plan, proposed by British Lord of the *Admiralty Winston Churchill*, called for an Allied fleet—mostly British—to force the *Dardanelles Strait* and then to steam to Constantinople to dictate peace terms. They began the campaign, convinced that the *Dardanelles* would fall in one month.

War Memorial at ANZAC Cove

This was the place where the *ANZAC (Australian and New Zealand Army Corps)* troops fought against the Turks and *Mustafa Kemal* proved himself as a real hero.

One year later, by contrast with the operation as a whole, the withdrawal was a masterpiece of planning and organization, with no loss of life. Estimates of Allied casualties for the entire campaign are about 252,000, with the Turks suffering almost as many casualties—an estimated 251,000.

< Wooden Horse, Troy

Common Words and Phrases

hello	*merhaba*	old	*eski*
good morning	*günaydın*	new	*yeni*
good day	*iyi günler*	very nice	*çok güzel*
good evening	*iyi akşamlar*	delicious	*lezzetli*
good night	*iyi geceler*		
good bye	*güle güle* (said by the one who stays)	this	*bu*
		that	*şu*
good bye	*hoşçakal* (said by the one who leaves)	restaurant	*lokanta*
		menu	*menü*
How are you?	*Nasılsınız?*	bill	*hesap*
I'm fine	*iyiyim*	tip	*bahşiş*
please	*lütfen*	VAT tax	*KDV*
thank you	*teşekkür (ederim), sağol*		
		salad	*salata*
Cheers!	*Şerefe!* (Literally "to your honor")	lemon	*limon*
		vinegar	*sirke*
Bon appétit	*Afiyet olsun*	oil	*yağ*
excuse me	*afedersiniz*	salt	*tuz*
okay	*tamam*	sugar	*şeker*
yes	*evet*	bread	*ekmek*
no	*hayır*	soup	*çorba*
no, none	*yok*	hot, spicy	*acı*
What is your name?	*Adın ne?*	tea	*çay*
My name is ...	*Adım ...*	apple tea	*elma çayı*
I / you / he, she, it	*ben / sen / o*	coffee	*kahve*
we / you / they	*biz / siz / onlar*	instant coffee	*neskafe*
How much is it?	*Ne kadar?*	decaffeinated	*kafeinsiz*
How many?	*Kaç tane?*	black coffee	*sade kahve*
cheap	*ucuz*	coffee with milk	*sütlü kahve*
expensive	*pahalı*	milk	*süt*

water	*su*	phone card	*telefon kartı*
bottled water	*şişe suyu*	token	*jeton*
fizzy mineral water	*soda, maden suyu*	taxi	*taksi*
beer	*bira*	ticket	*bilet*
whisky	*viski*		
gin and tonic	*cin tonik*	toilet	*tuvalet*
wine	*şarap*	woman	*bayan / kadın*
red wine	*kırmızı şarap*	man	*bay / erkek*
white wine	*beyaz şarap*		
		Help!	*İmdat!*
cold	*soğuk*	stop	*dur*
hot	*sıcak*		
ice	*buz*	lake	*göl*
spoon	*kaşık*	sea	*deniz*
fork	*çatal*	mountain	*dağ*
knife	*bıçak*	hill	*tepe*
glass	*bardak*	river	*nehir, akarsu*
plate	*tabak*	road	*yol*
		street	*cadde, sokak*
entrance	*giriş*		
exit	*çıkış*	student	*öğrenci*
		school	*okul*
hospital	*hastane*	primary school	*ilkokul*
insurance	*sigorta*	high school	*lise*
pharmacy	*eczane*	university	*üniversite*
medicine	*ilaç*	which grade?	*kaçıncı sınıf?*
post office	*postane (PTT)*	family	*aile*
letter	*mektup*	husband	*koca*
postcard	*kartpostal*	wife	*eş, hanım*
stamp	*pul*		

187

grandfather	*dede*
grandmother	*nine*
mother	*anne*
father	*baba*
son	*erkek çocuk*
daughter	*kız çocuk*
grandchild	*torun*
sister	*kızkardeş*
older sister	*abla*
brother	*erkek kardeş*
older brother	*ağabey, abi*
aunt (mother's sister)	*teyze*
aunt (father's sister)	*hala*
uncle (mother's brother)	*dayı*
uncle (father's brother)	*amca*
cousin	*kuzen*

house	*ev*
garden	*bahçe*
living room	*oturma odası*
bedroom	*yatak odası*
kitchen	*mutfak*
table	*masa*
chair	*sandalye*
fridge	*buzdolabı*
oven	*fırın*

How many children do you have?	*Kaç çocuğunuz var?*
How old are you?	*Kaç yaşındasınız?*
Where do you work? What is your job?	*Ne iş yapıyorsunuz?*
Is this yours?	*Bu sizin mi?*

NUMBERS

1	*bir*
2	*iki*
3	*üç*
4	*dört*
5	*beş*
6	*altı*
7	*yedi*
8	*sekiz*
9	*dokuz*
10	*on*
11	*onbir*
12	*oniki*
20	*yirmi*
21	*yirmibir*
30	*otuz*
40	*kırk*
50	*elli*
60	*altmış*
70	*yetmiş*
80	*seksen*
90	*doksan*
100	*yüz*
110	*yüzon*
200	*ikiyüz*

1,000	*bin*
2,000	*ikibin*
1,000,000	*milyon*
1,000,000,000	*milyar*

WEIGHTS AND MEASURES

The Metric and Kilo system is used.

Conversion Table

Temperature

°C > °F	multiply by 9, divide by 5, and add 32
°F > °C	subtract 32, multiply by 5, and divide by 9

Linear Measurement

1 centimeter	0.3937 inch
1 meter	3.280 feet
1 kilometer	0.6214 mile
1 inch	2.54 cm
1 foo	0.3048 m
1 yard	0.9144 m
1 mile	1.609 km

Mass

1 gram	15.43 grain
1 kilogram	2.205 pound
1 ton	2204.62 lb.
1 grain	64.8 mg
1 ounce	28.35 g
1 poun	0.4536 kg
1 stone	6.350 kg

Capacity Measurement

1 milliliter	0.00176 pint
1 liter	1.76 pint
1 fluid ounce	28.41 cm³
1 US gallon	3.785 dm³

Square Measurement

1 sq centimeter	0.1550 in²
1 sq meter	10.766 ft²
1 hectare	2.471 acres
1 sq kilometer	0.386 sq mile
1 square inch	645.16 mm²
1 square foot	0.0929 m²
1 square yard	0.8361 m²
1 acre	4047 m²
1 square mile	2.59 km²

Cubic Measurement

1 cubic centimeter	0.06102 in²
1 cubic meter	1.308 yd²
1 cubic inch	16.39 cm²
1 cubic foot	0.02832 m²
1 cubic yard	0.7646 m²

TIME

Local time is equal to **GMT + 2 hours**.
It is the same time zone all over the country.

ELECTRICITY

It is standard; **220 Volts** and **50 Hz** all over Turkey. Plugs suitable to Turkish standards have two round prongs.

TOURIST INFORMATION OFFICES

- *Atatürk Airport*
  212 - 465 3151

- *Sultanahmet-Hippodrome*
  Divan Yolu Cad. No: 5, Sultanahmet
  212 - 518 1802

- *Port of İstanbul*
  Karaköy Limanı Yolcu Salonu
  212 - 249 5776

- *Harbiye*
  Hilton Hotel Entrance
  212 - 233 0592

- *Bayezit Square*
  212 - 522 4902

- *Sirkeci Railway Station*
  212 - 511 5888

POSTAL SERVICES AND TELECOMMUNICATIONS

Turkey's postal services are comparatively organized and efficient. All post offices bear the distinctive yellow *PTT* sign (Post, Telephone, Telegrams). Larger and central offices are open from 8:00 AM-12:00 PM.

You can buy stamps in post offices. As a general rule, if you are not close to a post office, you can leave your postcards at hotel receptions with some cash; they will mail them for you. Mailing international postcards from Turkey is 0.80 TL. Prices for letters vary according to the size or weight; the starting fee is 0.85 TL.

www.ptt.gov.tr

Telephone

All cities are linked by an efficient direct dialing system. Public phones operate by *TT cards*, magnetic cards, credit cards or smart cards. These phones are available at public places such as squares, hospitals, bus terminals, train stations, seaports, airports, underground stations, etc. Cards are sold by Türk Telekom dealers. *TT cards* are calling cards that you can use from any phone.

The international country code for Turkey is **+90**. All over Turkey, phone numbers consist of two sections: area code (3 digits) and the number itself (7 digits).

The area code is **212 for the European side** of İstanbul and **216 for the Asian side**. Weekdays from 6:00 PM to 6:00 AM and on weekends, calls are cheaper than during business hours, and one can speak longer with the same amount of phone credit.

www.turktelekom.com.tr

Same area calls	→	just the 7 digit number
From area to area	→	0 + area code + number
International	→	0 + 0 + country code + area code + number

GSM Operators

- ***Turkcell***
  444 0532
  www.turkcell.com.tr/en

- ***Avea***
  444 1500
  www.avea.com.tr

- ***Vodafone***
  444 0542 (to call from abroad: +90 - 542 - 444 0542)
  www.vodafone.com.tr

Emergency & Useful Phone Numbers

İstanbul Directory	: 11811
Turkcell Directory	: 11832
Avea Directory	: 11855
Vodafone Directory	: 11842
Police	: 155
Traffic Police	: 154
Coastguard	: 158
Fire	: 110
Ambulance	: 112
Wake-up Calls	: 135

▌MONEY

The unit of currency is the *Turkish Lira (TL)*. Because of the high inflation until 2005 there were too many zeros in the currency; therefore, in 2005, six zeros were cancelled and the *New Turkish Lira (YTL)* was introduced. But after a few years the "new" has been eliminated again. The Turkish Lira (TL) banknotes and Kuruş (Kr) coins are officially in circulation as of January 1, 2009. In the meantime, Yeni Türk Lirası - The New Turkish Lira (YTL) banknotes and New Kuruş (YKr) coins are also valid until the end of 2009. The Turkish Lira is divided into 100 kuruş. Coins are 1, 5, 10, 25, 50 kuruş, and 1 lira. Bills or bank notes are 5, 10, 20, 50, 100, 200 liras.

You can legally use your foreign currencies in some places, such as the bazaar, etc. US Dollars and Euros are the most common. UK pounds sterling are less used. You may have difficulty with others.

It is always recommended that you have some Turkish currency with you for small restaurants, pharmacies, public restrooms, or grocery stores. If you want to pay in foreign currency in such places, you may experience difficulties with currency rates or change.

Using very large bills for small payments may make people unhappy. Therefore, it is recommended that you always pay with bills that are about equal to twice the amount of your purchase. This way you will always have smaller bills.

Banks and ATMs

Turkey boasts many banking companies, and branches can be found everywhere. The big retail banks all have ATMs, most of which give cash advances against foreign credit cards. It should be noted that most ATM entry codes use numbers rather than letters / passwords. While using ATMs, if anyone offers you any help, it is safer not to accept it. Banks will exchange foreign currency and traveler's checks with your passport as proof of identity. Commissions are charged at between 1 and 3% per transaction. Exchange rates change daily and can be checked in the press. Banks are usually open between 9:30 AM 12:00 AM and 1:30 PM 5:00 PM on weekdays. On Saturdays and Sundays they are closed.

Changing Money

"Döviz" or exchange offices offer fast service in and outside normal banking hours, and at better rates than banks or hotels. They have their buying and selling rates, and do not charge any commission and only change foreign cash currency. Passports are not required. In case you have any extra Turkish currency left with you before your departure, you can always change this into whichever currency you like at some change offices available at the airport. Exchange rates in Turkey are better than

the ones outside the country. Traveler's checks are becoming less efficient in Turkey. If you want to change traveler's checks, your two choices are banks or big hotels' receptions. Only a few change offices will accept traveler's checks. All of these places will charge a commission. In addition, you may have to wait in line and show your passport (not a copy) if you are at a bank. Therefore hotels' receptions are more practical.

- ### *Atatürk Commemoration, Youth and Sports Day (May 19)*
On this date in 1919, Mustafa Kemal first set foot on Anatolia at the Black Sea port of Samsun. This marks the beginning of his organization of the nationalist forces before the *Independence War*.

- ### *Victory Day (August 30)*
On this date in 1922, the fifth day of the big attack against the invading Greek troops, the *Dumlupınar Battle* under the command of Mustafa Kemal was won and determined the outcome of the *Independence War*. This big attack ended in Izmir with the defeat of the Greeks on September 9.

- ### *Republic Day (October 29)*
The Republic of Turkey was proclaimed by the *Turkish Grand National Assembly* in 1923.

Religious Holidays

There are two religious holidays or feasts: ***Şeker Bayramı (3 days)*** which comes immediately after 30 days of fasting in the holy month of Ramadan, and ***Kurban Bayramı (4 days)*** which follows 70 days after Seker Bayramı. In Turkish, ***Bayram*** is "feast" or "holiday", ***Şeker*** is "sweets" and ***kurban*** is a "sacrifice".

The dates of religious holidays come 10-11 days earlier each year because of the difference between the religious Lunar Year (354 days) and the Solar Year (365 days). Although not all the people in Anatolia are religious, these religious feasts are very traditional and have become essential. They are taken as seriously as Christmas is in the Christian world. People make lots of preparations in celebration of these feasts, such as cleaning houses, shopping, buying feast gifts, new clothes, sending greeting cards and so forth.

On the first day of the feast, very early in the morning, people get up, wash themselves, wear fragrance or cologne and put on their new clothes. The majority of the male population go to mosques for early morning prayer, as it is extremely important. School-aged children are also taken to mosques by their fathers or older relatives, in order to establish the habit of going to prayers. So many people go to mosques that they do not fit inside or even in the courtyard. When this is the case, they take small carpets from home to the mosque, put them in the streets near the mosque and join in with the service.

The Imams give sermons as this is an opportunity to preach to a large gathering. The dominant subject of the sermon in these days is peace. The Imams always try to encourage brotherhood and general goodwill among all. After prayers in the mosque, everybody gives the feast greeting to one another by shaking hands. The next stage is at home where feast greetings continue. In traditional extended families these greetings do not take too much time as all members are at the same place, but in nuclear families it might take a much longer time. Couples with their children visit their parents or grandparents, give gifts, kiss their hands, and eat candies or chocolates. Children are pleased as they are given some pocket money in addition to candies.

Another place that should not be missed is the cemetery, where the deceased members of the family are buried and need to be remembered. Flowers are taken and the soil of the grave is watered. Meanwhile family members read from the Koran in the name of the deceased.

The main visiting is over and now it is the time for some shopkeepers to open shops. Children are eager to spend their pocket money in grocery stores or amusement parks. In the following days, visits among friends, neighbors, and other relatives continue in a festive spirit. For people living far away from their families, feasts are a good reason to come together. Many people travel distances in order to make this possible.

Kurban Bayramı is the same as *Şeker Bayramı* except for the additional sacrifice, as the name of the feast implies.

The sacrificial animal (a ram, a goat, or any of the cattle) will be made ready for sacrifice. From the first morning onward, at anytime, it will be sacrificed by one of the members of the family or a representative of the family. The meat from the sacrificial animal is divided into three parts: one for the poor, one for the neighbors and relatives, and the last is for the family. The sacrificing is generally done in the courtyards of houses or if these do not exist then it is conducted in specially arranged public places. Instead of actually making the sacrifice, people may make a donation of the same value to a charity.

WORKING HOURS

- **Government offices:** 8:30 AM - 12:30 PM; 1:30 PM - 5:30 PM (Closed on Saturdays and Sundays)
- **Banks:** 8:30 AM - 12:00 PM; 1:30 PM - 5:00 PM (Closed on Saturdays and Sundays)
- **Shops:** 9:30 AM - 7:00 PM (In tourist areas, closing times vary, some will close around midnight)
- **Grand Bazaar & Spice Bazaar:** 8:00 AM - 7:00 PM (Closed on Sundays)
- **Modern Shopping Malls:** 10:00 AM - 10:00 PM
- **Museums:** 9:00 AM - 5:00 PM (Most of them are closed on Mondays)
- **Pharmacies:** 9:00 AM - 7:00 PM (Closed on Sundays and holidays)

NEWSPAPERS

For international news, major papers are delayed reaching Turkey, but the *Herald Tribune* is printed in Turkey and easier to find. For local news in English you can follow *Today's Zaman, Turkish Daily News* daily. You can find these papers at major newspaper stands or you can read them at their websites.

www.todayszaman.com
www.turkishdailynews.com.tr

TOILETS

Toilets may be oriental or western style. They have separate sections for men and women. Near each mosque, in each museum there are usually public toilets. Small water pipes

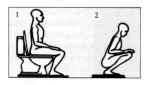

coming from the back of the toilets are for water to cleanse with providing a simplified bidet. Toilet paper is used just for drying. Therefore, since paper is not thought to be absolutely necessary, you might not find enough toilet paper in all public facilities. Public toilets are always better in hotels and restaurants. Some public toilets in more traditional places may be primitive. In most places people have to pay to use public facilities.

INTERNET CAFES

Most hotels offer Internet services, some of which are free.
Most hotels will offer wireless connection, especially in public
areas, at no charge. In addition to hotels, you can use Internet
cafes. You should note the two different characters for "i" in
the Turkish alphabet: "i, İ" and "ı, I". Especially while using the
Internet, if one character does not work, try the other. What
you see on the screen is the correct one.

The "@" sign may sometimes be difficult to find. In most
Turkish keyboards you can get the "@" sign by pressing the
"Alt Gr" and "Q" together.

SAFETY

Pickpockets

İstanbul is one of the largest cities in the world and although the crime rate is not so high in comparison with other large cities, the number of pickpockets is increasing. Even on a main street during the day pickpockets may be working. The most common ploy is a staged fight among a few young teen-aged boys. One of them may hide behind you and the others will try to get him. During this skirmish they may empty your pockets or grab ladies' purses. Therefore, it is always necessary to be careful.

Offers for Help

Never let strangers lead you to a shop, a bar, a restaurant or a nightclub. What they do is not legal. You may meet people of this kind on a corner, in the street, or even in the hotel lobby. They may be well dressed and able to speak good English; they may even tell you they work at the hotel and that they know you from the hotel. Although it does not mean that every offer will end with a rip-off, we do like to discourage such activities.

ANTIQUITIES

From time to time genuine antiquities as well as imitations are offered for sale. Under no circumstance should these be purchased. Their sale, purchase, or possession is strictly controlled by Turkish Law, and punishments are severe. For instance, to take an old carpet or an old piece of copper out of the country, one has to get approval from the directorate of an authorized museum. Dealers generally provide it.

DRUGS

The possession, sale, or use of drugs such as hashish, heroin, or cocaine is illegal and strictly forbidden by Turkish Law.

TAKING PHOTOS

In Security Areas
Photography is not permitted in places such as docks, airports, military establishments, frontier areas, etc. Check for signs or ask for advice if uncertain.

In the Museums
Some museums will not allow photography at all or may ask you to buy a ticket for your camera. In most museums, you will be able to take photos without using any flash or a tripod. Always look for the signs.

Of People
Asking for permission or at least gesturing that you would like permission will provide you with a positive response in most cases. If you catch a photo of someone, he/she will sometimes ask you to mail it to him/her and will give you his/her address. To do so would bring pleasure to the person.

PLACES OF WORSHIP

Mosques
Almost 98-99% of the population is Moslems, majority of which are Sunnis. Functioning mosques are all around. There is no membership system in Islam so people can go to whichever mosques they like.

Synagogues
To visit synagogues in İstanbul, you must make reservations one day ahead of time. Fax your message using the letterhead of your hotel and attach copies of your passports. The next day take your passports with you. Call 212 - 293 8794 to get general information.

Synagogues

Neve Shalom Synagogue
Büyük Hendek Cad,
No: 67 Şişhane - Karaköy
212 - 292 0386

Etz-Ahayim Synagogue
Muallim Naci Sk,
No: 40/41, Ortaköy
212 - 260 1896

Ahrida Synagogue
Kürkçü Çeşme Cad,
No: 9 Balat
212 - 523 7407

Bet Yaakov Synagogue
İcadiye Cad, No: 9
Kuzguncuk
212 - 243 5166

No synagogue visits on Saturday and Sunday

Catholic Churches

Cathedral Saint Esprit
Cumhuriyet Cad,
No: 205/B, Harbiye
212 - 248 0910
Everyday: 6:00 PM,
Sunday: 9:00 AM, 10:15 AM,
11:15 AM (in French
and English)

St. Anthony of Padua
İstiklal Cad, No: 225, Beyoğlu
212 - 244 0935
Everyday: 08:00 AM English,
07:00 PM Turkish
Sunday: 09:30 AM Polish,
10:00 AM English,
11:30 AM Italian

Saint George
Kart Çınar Sk, No: 10, Karaköy
212 - 244 1882
Sunday 10:00 AM

Saint Paul
Cumhuriyet Cad, Selbaşı Sk,
No: 5 Harbiye -Taksim
212 - 248 3691
Sunday: 11:30 AM

Santa Maria Draperies
İstiklal Cad, No: 429, Beyoğlu
212 - 244 0243
Everyday: 8:00 AM,
Friday & Saturday: 5:00 PM,
Sunday: 9:00 AM, 11:30 AM,
5:00 PM

Protestant Churches

Christ Church
Serdar Ekrem Sk, No: 82
Tünel - Beyoğlu
212 - 251 5616
Everyday: 9:00 AM, 6:00 PM,
Sunday: 10:00 AM

Union Church
Dutch Consulate,
Postacılar Sk, No: 11, Beyoğlu
212 - 244 5212
Sunday 9:30 AM, 11:00 AM,
1:30 PM

Orthodox Churches

**(Greek) St. George Fener
Patriarch Church**
Sadrazam Ali Paşa Cad, No: 35
Fener - Eyüp
212 - 531 9670 -76

(Greek) Hagia Triada
Meşelik Sk, No: 11/1, Taksim
212 - 244 1358
Sunday: 09:00 AM

**(Syrian) Orthodox Churches
Church of the Virgin Mary**
Karakurum Sk, No: 20
Tarlabaşı - Beyoğlu

**(Russian) Orthodox Churches
Andrievskaya Church**
Mumhane Cad, No: 63
Karaköy

**(Russian) on the Athos
St. Panteleimon Monastery**
Hoca Tahsın Sk, No:19/6
Karaköy

Armenian Churches

Armenian Patriarchate
Şarapnel Sk, No: 3, Kumkapı
212 - 517 0970

Surp Kirkor Lusavoric
Sakızcılar Sk, No: 3, Karaköy
212 - 292 5762
Thursday: 09:30 AM

Üç Horan
Balık Pazarı, Beyoğlu
212 - 244 1382
Everyday: 09:00 AM -12:00 PM

Consulates

• **Australia**
Ritz Carlton 2nd floor
Asker Ocağı Cad, No: 15, Elmadağ
212 - 243 1333

• **Austria**
Köybaşı Cad, No: 46, Yeniköy
212 - 363 8410

• **Belgium**
Sıraselviler Cad, No: 73, Taksim
212 - 243 3300

• **Brazil**
Basın Ekspres Yolu, Kavak Sk. No: 3
Eresinler Ser Plaza A Blok Kat: 3
Yenibosna
0212 - 652 1000

• **Bulgaria**
Ulus Mah. Ahmet Adnan Saygun Cad.
No: 44, 2. Levent
212 - 281 0115

• **Canada**
İstiklal Cad. No: 373/5, Beyoğlu
212 - 251 9838

• **China**
Memduh Paşa Yalısı, Kireçburnu Mah.
Mısırlı Cad. Tarabya
212 - 299 2188

• **Czech Republic**
Abdi İpekçi Cad. No: 71, Maçka
212 - 230 9597

• **Denmark**
Meygede Sk. No: 2, Bebek
212 - 359 1900

• **Egypt**
Konaklar Mah. Akasyalı Sk. No: 26
4. Levent
212 - 324 2160

• **Finland**
Cumhuriyet Cad. No: 111, K: 8
Elmadağ - Harbiye
212 - 296 9549

• **France**
İstiklal Cad. No: 8, Taksim
212 - 334 8730

• **Germany**
İnönü Cad. No: 16, Gümüşsuyu
212 - 334 6100

• **Greece**
Turnacıbaşı Sk. No: 32
Galatasaray - Beyoğlu
212 - 393 8290, 212 - 245 0597 - 98

• **Hungary**
Metrocity, A Blok, 6th floor, Levent
212 - 344 1265 - 67

• **India**
Cumhuriyet Cad. No: 18, Harbiye
212 - 296 2132

• **Iran**
Ankara Cad. No: 1/2, Cağaloğlu
212 - 513 8230 - 32

• **Israel**
Büyükdere Cad. Yapı Kredi Plaza
C Blok, 4. Levent
212 - 317 6500

• **Italy**
Boğazkesen Cad.Tomtom Kaptan Sk.
No: 15, Galatasaray - Beyoğlu
212 - 243 1024-25

• **Japan**
Tekfen Tower, Büyükdere Cad.
No: 209, 10th floor, 4.Levent
212 - 317 4600

• **Lebanon**
Teşvikiye Cad. Saray Apt
No:134/1, Saray Apt. Teşvikiye
212 - 236 1365

• **Mexico**
Teşvikiye Cad No: 107/2, Teşvikiye
212 - 227 3500

• **Netherlands**
İstiklal Cad. No: 197, Beyoğlu
212 - 393 2121

• **New Zealand**
İnonü Cad. No: 48
Mithatpaşa Apt. K:2 D:3 Taksim
212 - 244 0272

• **Norway**
Bilezik Sk. No: 4, Fındıklı
212 - 249 9753

• **Portugal**
Meclisi Mebusan Cad. No: 77 K: 5
Fındıklı - Kabataş
212 - 251 9118

• **Romania**
Sıraselviler Cad. No: 55, Taksim
212 - 292 4126, 212 - 244 4284

• **Russia**
İstiklal Cad. No: 443, Beyoğlu
212 - 292 5101

• **Singapore**
Kazım Özalp Sk. No: 28/8
Ethem Bey Apt. K: 3, Şaşkınbakkal
216 - 358 0133

• **South Africa Republic (Honorary)**
Muallim Naci Cad. No: 69, Ortaköy
212 - 227 5200

• **Spain**
Karanfil Aralığı Sk. No: 16, 1. Levent
212 - 270 7410

• **Sweden**
İstiklal Cad. No: 497, Tünel
212 - 334 0600

• **Switzerland**
Büyükdere Cad. No: 173, Levent
212 - 283 1282

• **Syria**
Maçka Cad. No: 59/3, Teşvikiye
212 - 232 6721

• **Turkish Republic of Northern Cyprus**
Yeni Gelin Sk. No: 24/1
Balmumcu, Beşiktaş
212 - 227 3490

• **United Arab Emirates**
Konaklar Mah. Büyükdere Cad.
Meşeli Sk. No:11, 4. Levent
212 - 279 6348

• **United Kingdom**
Meşrutiyet Cad. No: 34, Tepebaşı
212 - 334 6400

• **USA**
İstinye Mah. Kaplıcalar Mevkii Sk.
No: 2, İstinye
212 - 335 9000

▌ MOVIES ABOUT İSTANBUL BY FOREIGNERS*

- "Die Nacht der Grossen Liebe" directed by
  *Geza von Bolvary (Jarmila Novotna,
  Gustav Fröhlich, Fritz Odemar)*
  Germany (1933)

- "The Mask of Dimitrios" directed by *Jean
  Negulesco (Sydney Greenstreet, Zachary
  Scott, Faye Emerson, Peter Lorre)*
  USA (1944)

- "Tintin et le mystère de la Toison d'Or"
  directed by *Jean-Jacques Vierne (Georges
  Wilson, Jean-Pierre Talbot, Dario Moreno,
  Charles Vanel)* France/Belgium (1961)

- "L'Immortelle" directed by *Alain Robbe-
  Grillet (Françoise Brion, Jacques Doniol-Val
  croze, Guido Celano, Sezer Sezin, Ulvi Uraz)*
  France/Italy (1962)

- "From Russia with Love" directed by
  *Terence Young (Sean Connery, Daniela
  Bianchi, Pedro Armendariz, Robert Shaw)*
  England (1963)

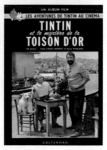

- "Topkapı" directed by *Jules Dassin
  (Melina Mercouri, Peter Ustinov,
  Maximilian Schell, Robert Morley)*
  USA (1964)

- "La Corne d'Or" directed by *Maurice Pialat*,
  France (1964) - Documentary

---

* This list has primarily been prepared by Giovanni Scognamillo.

- "Estanbul 65/That Man in İstanbul" directed by *Antonio İsasi İsasmendi (Horst Bucholtz, Sylva Koscina, Klaus Kinsky)* Spain/Italy/France (1965)

- "Les Deux Reporters Autour du Monde" directed *Claude Boissol (Gillian Hills, Edouard Meeks, Regnier)* France (1965) – İstanbul section of the TV series

- "Murder on the Orient Express" directed by *Sidney Lumet (Albert Finney, Lauren Bacall, Martin Balsam, Ingrid Bergman, Jacqueline Bisset)* USA (1974)

- "Le Orme" directed by *Luigi Bazzoni and Mario Fanelli (Florinda Boklan, Peter McEnery, Lila Kedrova, Klaus Kinsky)* Italy (1975)

- "Le Reve d'Esther" directed by *Jacques Otmezguine (Ludmilla Mikael, Sam Karman, Lisa Martino, Işık Aras)* France (1994) – TV

- "Hamam – Bagno Turco" directed
  by Ferzan Özpetek (Alessandro Gassman,
  Francesca d'Aloja, Carlo Cecchi)
  Italy (1997)

- "James Bond 007: The World Is Not
  Enough" directed by *Michael Apted*
  (Pierce Brosnan, Sophie Marceau,
  Robert Carlyle, Denise Richards)
  USA (1999)

- "Crossing the Bridge: The Sound of
  İstanbul" directed by *Fatih Akin*
  (Alexander Hacke, Baba Zula, Orient
  Expressions, Duman, Replikas,
  Erkin Koray) 2005

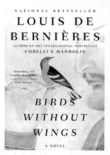

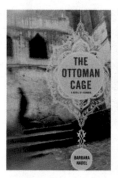

BOOKS ABOUT İSTANBUL BY FOREIGNERS

- "Aziyade" by the French novelist *Pierre Loti*
- "Murder on the Orient Express" (Hercule Poirot Mysteries) by British Writer *Agatha Christie*
- "From Russia with Love" by British Novelist *Ian Fleming*
- "The Ottoman Cage: A Novel of Istanbul" by English Crime-Writer *Barbara Nadel*
- "Arabesk" by English Crime-Writer *Barbara Nadel*
- "Turkish Embassy Letters" by English Writer *Lady Mary Wortley Montagu*
- "Turkish Reflections: Biography of a Place" by American Writer *Mary Lee Settle*
- "Birds Without Wings" by English Writer *Louis de Bernieres*
- "Tales from the Expat Harem: Foreign Women in Modern Turkey"
- "Ataturk: A Biography of Mustafa Kemal, Father of Modern Turkey" by Scottish P*atrick Balfour Kinross* and *Lord Kinross*
- "The Turkish Letters" *by Flemish Writer and Diplomat Ogier Ghiselin de Busbecq* (Imperial Ambassador at Constantinople, 1554-1562)
- "Eothen: Traces of Travel Brought Home from the East" by *English Writer and Historian Alexander William Kinglake*
- "The Owl's Watchsong a Study of İstanbul" by *English Writer J.A. Cuddon* and *Derrick Greaves*
- "A Byzantine Journey" by *Expatriate British Writer John Ash*

▌BY AIR

National carrier of Turkey is Turkish Airlines with regular flights
to almost all major countries. Most of the major international
airlines as well as charters fly into İstanbul. The two international airports are Atatürk and Sabiha Gökçen. Atatürk Airport
is the largest and busiest in Turkey. It is on the European side
of İstanbul and close to the major centers such as the Old City
and the Taksim Square. Depending on the traffic, it will take
between 30-60 minutes to get there. Almost all of the major
airlines use this airport. Sabiha Gökçen Airport is on the Asian
side of İstanbul. It will take between 1-2 hours to get to major
parts of the city.

- **Atatürk Airport**
212 - 465 5555
www.ataturkairport.com

- **Sabiha Gökçen Airport**
216 - 585 5000
www.sgairport.com

- **Airport - City Lines (Havaş)**
212 - 444 0487
www.havas.com.tr

Atatürk Airport - Taksim
There are shuttles in every half hour between 04:00 AM and 01:00 AM Each ride takes approximately 40 minutes if there is no heavy traffic. Drop-off points are Bakırköy Sea Bus Pier, Aksaray and Tepebaşı.

Sabiha Gökçen Airport - Taksim
Shuttles from the airport will be available after each arrival. Shuttles from Taksim are daily at 03:30 AM, 04:30 AM, 05:30 AM, 06:30 AM, 07:30 AM, 08:30 AM, 09:30 AM, 11:30 AM, 12:30 PM, 1:30 PM, 2:30 PM, 3:30 PM, 4:30 PM, 5:30 PM, 6:30 PM, 7:30 PM, 8:30 PM, 10:00 PM and 12:00 AM. Each ride will take approximately one hour.

212 - 444 0487
www.havas.com.tr

BY SEA

Many cruise ships in the Aegean Sea reach İstanbul. For some of them İstanbul is the turn around port. A regular ferry service between İstanbul and Ukraine is available.

- *Karaköy Sea Port*
  212 - 249 5776, 212 - 245 5366, 212 - 249 71 78

- *Turkish Maritime Authority*
  212 - 251 5000, 212 - 243 6873

BY RAIL

It is possible to get to İstanbul (Sirkeci) from Sofia, Belgrade, Bucharest and Budapest. Vienna and Munich connections are available too.

There are two railway stations in İstanbul:

- *Haydarpaşa Railway Station (Asian side)*
  216 - 336 4470, 216 - 337 8724

- *Sirkeci Railway Station (European side)*
  212 - 520 6575 ext. 417

< *Haydarpaşa Railway Station*

SMART TICKET *(AKBİL)* & OTHERS

Each ticket is very reasonably priced; one-way transportation is approximately more than one American Dollar. When using public transportation in the city, you have two choices:

1. You can buy a one-time-use ticket, five-time use *"Beşibiryerde"* or token before you board a vehicle except for public buses. You need to get

them before you board. They are available at ticket booths. Use it at the entrance to the vehicle or in the station. The five-time use *"Beşibiryerde"* electronic ticket cards can be used only for the public buses.

2. You can purchase an *Akbil*-Smart Ticket. The *Akbil* method is widely used on İstanbul's public transportation, but may not be used for *dolmuş*es or taxis. *The Seasonal Blue Akbil* is available in daily, weekly and 15-day formats. You can see the expiration date and time of your *Akbil* by touching it to credit sockets available on the vehicle, at stops, or in stations.

For timetables and lines, etc., you can always check www.istanbul-ulasim.com.tr

PUBLIC BUSES

Buses are widely used all over the city. A 24-hour call center is available at 444 0088. To see which line goes where and timetables, you can visit the website:

www.iett.gov.tr/en/saat/hareketsaati

SUBWAY *(METRO)*

a

The subway system in İstanbul is brand new, in operation only since 2000. It started at *Taksim Square* and reached the last stop of *4. Levent* (6 stops in total). Total length of the line was only 8.5 km (5.2 miles). Each ride was 12 minutes and it operated every 5-7 minutes between 6:15 AM. and 12:30 AM.

b

The *Taksim-Şişhane* line (1.65 km/ 1 mile) and the *4. Levent-Maslak Atatürk Oto Sanayi* line (5.5 km - 3.4 miles) have just been added. It will continue to grow.

TRAM *(HIZLI TRAMVAY)*

The electric tram is very efficient especially in the old city section. It starts in *Kabataş* and by crossing the *Galata Bridge* on the *Golden Horn*, reaches the *Blue Mosque* and the *Grand Bazaar*. One of the lines reaches the airport as well, but the line has to be changed at one of the crossroads.

c

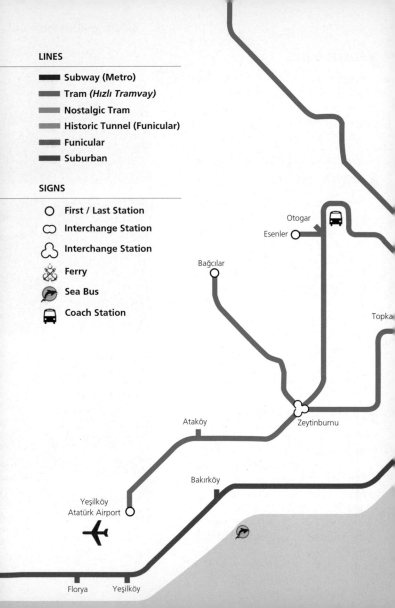

LINES

- **Subway (Metro)**
- **Tram** (*Hızlı Tramvay*)
- **Nostalgic Tram**
- **Historic Tunnel (Funicular)**
- **Funicular**
- **Suburban**

SIGNS

- ○ First / Last Station
- ◯ Interchange Station
- ⬡ Interchange Station
- ⚹ Ferry
- ◉ Sea Bus
- 🚌 Coach Station

Otogar

Esenler ○

Bağcılar ○

Topka[pı]

Ataköy

Zeytinburnu

Bakırköy

Yeşilköy
Atatürk Airport ○

Florya   Yeşilköy

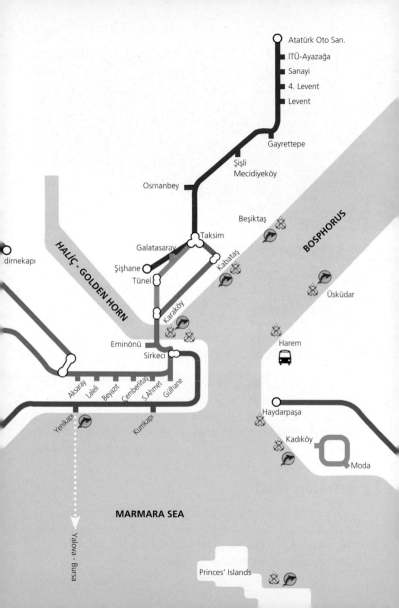

FUNICULAR

The funicular is a relatively new means of transportation that connects *Taksim Square* to *Kabataş*, the Subway to the Tram. It is only one stop and takes less than 3 minutes. It uses the subway station in *Taksim Square*.

TARİHİ TÜNEL - HISTORIC TUNNEL (FUNICULAR)

This is the old funicular that has been named ***Tarihi Tünel*** (Historic Tunnel) since the time it was started in 1875. It is among the oldest subways in the world and has recently been renovated. It operates between *İstiklal Street* and *Karaköy* with only one stop, and takes less than 3 minutes.

NOSTALGIC TRAM

This is the two-car tram operating in the pedestrian street of İstiklal between *Taksim Square* and *Tünel*. It moves very slowly and gives you the chance to enjoy observing life on *İstiklal Street*. It stops at *Galatasaray* mid-way.

Nostalgic Tram at the İstiklal Street >

▌FERRY
(*ŞEHİR HATLARI VAPURLARI*)

The busy city of İstanbul sits on the shores of Europe and Asia. Many of the inhabitants live on one continent but work, study or socialize on the other. Apart from the two bridges on the Bosphorus, ferries are the only means to connect the two continents and are therefore vital.

You can use Smart Ticket *Akbil* or need to buy a token at the entrance to the Ferry Station

To see the routes and timetables, you can click on the "Conventional Ferry Timetables" at <u>www.ido.com.tr</u>

Major Ferry Lines:
- Karaköy-Haydarpaşa-Kadıköy
- Eminönü-Üsküdar
- Eminönü-Kadıköy
- Kabataş-Kadıköy
- Kabataş-Princes' Islands
- Beşiktaş-Üsküdar
- Beşiktaş-Kadıköy
- Eminönü-Bosphorus
- Bostancı-Princes' Islands

SEA BUS
(DENİZ OTOBÜSLERİ)

In addition to the ferry system, these fast and smooth services by air conditioned power boats offer very efficient commuting from one point to another across the Bosphorus. They are more expensive than the regular public ferries.

You can use Smart Ticket **Akbil** or need to buy a token at the entrance to the Sea Bus Station.

Call center: 212 - 444 4436
An efficient website with online reservation service:
www.ido.com.tr

Major Sea Bus Lines:
- Bakırköy-Yenikapı-Kadıköy-Bostancı
- Kabataş-Bostancı
- Kabataş-Princes' Islands
(Kınalı-Burgaz-Heybeli-Büyükada)-Bostancı
- Sarıyer-Beykoz-İstinye-Beşiktaş-Kabataş-Kadıköy

- Bostancı-Yalova-Kartal
- Pendik-Kartal-Maltepe
- Bakırköy-Avcılar

- Yenikapı-Yalova
- Pendik-Yalova
- Yenikapı-Bandırma
- Yenikapı-Bursa

TAXI *(TAKSİ)*

Taxis are numerous all over the city and are recognizable by their yellow color and lighted **"TAKSİ"** signs on top. Each taxi is metered and there are two different rates. The starting fee in the meter is 2.00 Turkish Liras. It will be 3.00 TL after midnight until 6.00 a.m. as it is 50% higher for the night shift. The fees are per cab, not per person. Additional expenses such as ferryboat or bridge crossing fees are extra to passengers. Tipping is not necessary, but leaving the change or rounding up the fare is customary.

To avoid any possible trouble, instead of using the taxis that are waiting at the corner of the *Grand Bazaar* or the *Topkapı Palace*, take a taxi which is passing by. If they do not start the meter, take another one. Before you make your payment, just to be on the safe side, please get out of the taxi first and then while paying with one hand, receive the change with your other hand so that your big bill is not exchanged for a smaller one.

DOLMUŞ

Dolmuş (literally, full of passengers) is a kind of shared taxi, which may be a large car, a station wagon, a regular taxi, or a minibus. It follows a specific fixed route. Passengers pay according to the distance traveled and can get in and out whenever and wherever they want by informing the driver. It is a very practical means of transport and much cheaper than a taxi. The *dolmuş* fares are determined by distances, and set by the municipalities.

█ *DOLMUŞ* BOATS *(DOLMUŞ MOTOR)*

This is the sea version of the regular land *dolmuş*es. They are
efficiently used to cross the Bosphorus between the European
and Asian parts of İstanbul. The most popular dolmuş boat
stations are *Beşiktaş, Kabataş, Kadıköy* and *Üsküdar.*

LIMOUSINE SERVICES

• afm Limousine
Nispetiye Cad. Peker Sk.
No: 4/1, 1. Levent
212 - 325 4717
www.afmlimousine.com

• Inter Limousine Service
Cemal Reşit Rey
Konser Salonu Altı,
Inter Kat Otoparkı,
Harbiye
212 - 444 9977
www.interlimousine.com.tr

• DTLS Limousine
Emirhan Cad. 7/17
Beşiktaş
212 - 258 9125
www.dtlstravel.com

• Yaşaroğlu Limousine
İnönü Mah. Ölçek Sk.
No: 121, Harbiye
212 - 225 3243
www.yasaroglulimousine.com

AIRCRAFT & HELICOPTER CHARTERS

• Fly Medair
212 - 335 8570
Reservation
212 - 234 7777
www.flymedair.com

• Sancak Air
212 - 541 4141-3
www.sancakair.com.tr

• Top Air
212 - 465 4866 - 7
212 - 624 9819
www.topair.com.tr

• Jet Partner
212 - 465 7560
532 - 565 9995
www.jetpartner.com.tr

• Bon Air
212 - 663 1829
www.bonair.com.tr

CAR RENTAL

• *Decar*
212 - 337 3949
www.decar.com.tr

• *Europecar*
216 - 427 0427
www.europcar.com.tr

• *Avis*
212 - 444 2847
www.avis.com.tr

• *Budget*
216 - 444 4722
www.trbudget.com

TÜRSAB (The Association of Turkish Travel Agencies)

The Association of Turkish Travel Agencies is a professional organization with legal status, established by Law in 1972.

The main aims of the Association are:
1) Develop the travel agency profession in harmony with the country's economy and tourism sector.
2) Protect professional ethics and solidarity.

In accordance with Law #1618, a travel agency can be established only upon the issuance of a license by the Ministry of Culture and Tourism. The agency is then obliged to become a member of *TÜRSAB* in order to conduct travel agency business and offer the services specified by this law.

Travel agencies that are members of *TÜRSAB* can provide all kinds of services for organizing tours, meetings, or conferences, and the issuance of air tickets. For a list of member travel agencies, you can take a look at the *TÜRSAB* website.

Dikilitaş, Aşık Kerem Sk.
No: 42, Beşiktaş
212 - 259 8404
www.tursab.org.tr

ORGANIZED TOURS

- **Plan Tours**
212 - 234 7777
212 - 230 2272
www.plantours.com

- **Popular Tours - ITS**
212 - 275 1870
www.dailycitytours.com

AIR SIGHTSEEING WITH HELICOPTER

- **Plan Tours**
212 - 234 7777
212 - 230 2272
www.plantours.com

OPEN-TOP DOUBLE DECKER

Sightseeings with open-top double deckers. Hop on and hop off possibilities are available.

- **İstanbul Vision Daily Panoramic Tour**
212 - 234 7777
212 - 230 2272
www.plantours.com

PRIVATE TOURIST GUIDES

Turkish tourist guides rank among the best in the world. They are mostly knowledgeable and accommodating. You can hire a guide directly. To see a list of guides: www.turkishguides.org

Please check if your tourist guide is licensed! Unqualified guiding is illegal in Turkey. For consumer rights always ask for licensed guides. All licensed tourist guides must wear their official badges during tours.

Shopping

İstanbul is a treasure trove for shoppers, especially those who are interested in the local culture and want the opportunity to interact with local people and take part in their customs. İstanbul offers many unique and interesting things to buy, and, of course, tourists' purchases contribute a great deal to the local economy.

You can always try bargaining in the bazaars, etc. Even in a modern store where prices are marked, you may try bargaining politely by asking if it is their best price. Please bear in mind that if you offer a price for an item, and it is agreed upon, you will be expected to buy it. As a general rule, be happy with your bargain and don't compare prices later.

WHAT TO BUY

• *Carpets & Kilims* *

A carpet is more a work of art than an article that people walk on for everyday use.

Seventy percent of tourists coming to Turkey return home with carpets because Turkey is a treasure house of carpets.

To understand how valuable Turkish carpets are, one must go back to their origin. For a nomad who lived in a tent, home was a simple place: a combination of walls, roof and floor. The floor was just a simple carpet laid directly onto the earth.

The carpet was a bug-excluder, soil leveler, temperature controller and comfort provider all in one. The texture of the material beneath one's feet was sensual proof that this was home and not the wild.

> #### *Shopping in the Street*
>
> Street vendors sell a lot of things, such as, disposable t-shirts or fake perfumes; but, sometimes they may be selling something interesting, such as, a good picture book or sets of postcards. The vendors may be insistent. If you show attention to them, they will keep bothering you. If you are not interested, you should avoid eye contact.

* Norman Roger, *Newspot*, 1995/2

Historically, there are fragments that exist from the 5-6C AD, but it is from the *Seljuk* period in *Anatolia* that many pieces have survived. *Marco Polo*, during his journey through *Seljuk* lands toward the end of the 13C reported that the best and finest carpets were produced in Konya.

Since a carpet is more of a work of art, the deeper meanings of each design should not be neglected. A carpet can be likened to a poem; neither can tolerate any extra element that does not contribute to its wholeness and value. Therefore, just as in a poem, a carpet pattern is chosen for its beauty, and the motifs are carefully arranged to form rhymes.

Turkish carpets carry a wide range of symbols. For many centuries, Anatolian women expressed their wishes, fears, interests, fidelity, and love through the artistic medium of carpets; nevertheless, there are typically repeated motifs which vary from region to region: geometric, tree of life, central medallion, prayer niches in prayer rugs, etc.

Turkish carpets are made of silk, wool or cotton. A silk pile gives a carpet great brilliance. Cotton-warped carpets almost always have a more rigid and mechanical appearance than woolen-warped. Yarns are used in their natural colors or colored with dyes extracted from flowers, roots and insects.

Carpets are made on vertical looms strung with 3 to 24 warp (vertical) threads per cm (8 to 60 per in) of width.

Working from bottom to top, the carpet maker either weaves the rug with a flat surface or knots it for a pile texture. Pile rugs use 5-7.5 cm / 2-3 in lengths of yarn tied in Turkish *(Gördes)* or Persian *(Sehna)* knots with rows of horizontal weft yarn laced over and under the vertical warp threads for strength. After the carpet is completely knotted, its pile is sheared and the warp threads at each end are tied into a fringe. The finer the yarn and the closer the warp threads are strung together, the denser the weave and, usually, the finer the quality.

The best-known flat-woven rug is the kilim that is lighter in weight and less bulky than pile rugs. It has a plain weave made by shooting the weft yarn over and under the warp threads in one row, then alternating the weft in the next row. The *sumak* type is woven in a herringbone pattern by wrapping a continuous weft around pairs of warp threads.

Taking a tour of a carpet production center is highly recommended in order to have a firsthand learning experience of this art and to see a full range of the different designs exhibited.

• Tiles & Ceramics

İznik (Nicaea) was the largest tile production center during the Ottoman period. The *İznik* tiles were different from *Seljuk* tiles in color and quality.

According to the records of 17C traveler *Evliya Çelebi*, there were 340 ateliers of tiles in İznik when he visited there. When an *Ottoman* **Sultan** wanted to build a new building, he sent a message to the governor of İznik. All the work was distributed to the ateliers. Tiles used for interior decorations were 24x24 cm / 9.45x9.45 in and 2-3 cm / 0.7x1.2 in thick. In the beginning of the 16C, motifs on tiles had blue, dark blue and yellow colors on white background. In the second half of the century more motifs were used and color combinations became more complex. A certain shade of coral that was first seen in the middle of the 16C suddenly disappeared in the 17C, which can only be explained with the death of its master.

By the 18C, the ceramic industry in İznik had died out completely and Kütahya replaced it as the leading center in western *Anatolia*.

For a while, the Kütahya potters produced inferior copies of İznik blue-and-whites but they also began producing ceramics whose forms, colors, and techniques were quite distinct. There is a third important group of Turkish ceramics that is quite different from both the products of İznik and Kütahya. Çanakkale ceramics have begun to attract the interest and attention of researchers and collectors more and more in recent years.

To summarize, the art of Turkish tile and the making of ceramics developed over the centuries incorporating many different techniques and styles. Enriched by the arrival of the *Seljuks*, the ceramic industry in *Anatolia* achieved a deservedly worldwide reputation with the support of the *Ottoman Court*. Today, Kütahya has revived as an important center for the making of tile and ceramics. In addition, efforts are also being made in private workshops and educational institutions in İznik, İstanbul, and Bursa to keep the art of traditional Turkish tiles and ceramics alive and develop it so that it can meet the demands of modern-day life.

• **Calligraphy**

Calligraphy (from Gr. meaning "beautiful writing") is the art of fine handwriting. The term may refer to letters, words, pages, or even whole documents to which aesthetic principles and skilled penmanship have been applied. In Islamic culture, calligraphic writing is accomplished by using a broad-edged reed, quill, or nib pen held at a slant.

In a country where Islam is practiced, calligraphy is of great importance since depictions of humans and animals are not allowed. The copying of the *Koran* is considered a religious act and Islamic calligraphy is much esteemed because of its religious associations. Major styles of script are *Kufi*, a formal style with an angular character, *Sülüs*, a cursive flowing script written with rounded letters, *Divani*, generally used for writing the decrees, and Talik. These scripts are also classified in themselves according to the places that they are used or their sizes.

• *Marbled Paper (Ebru)*

Ebru is a traditional Turkish art. Although the origins are unknown, it is likely that it came to *Anatolia* from Central Asia. Natural dyes mixed with ox gall are sprinkled with horse hair brushes upon the surface of water in a deep ebru tray. The oily dyes are designed on the surface of the water. After the design is ready, tray-size papers are left on the tray to absorb all the dyes as they are, with their formed shape.

Ebru is an abstract art in which a considerable amount of randomness is involved. The artist's control is decidedly limited as he cannot determine the precise shape, size or position of each droplet of color. What he does is to try to apply his colors according to the "mood" of the ebru tray as he perceives it. The colors then float and expand depending on the condition of the liquid and the tray, the ambient temperature, the humidity and the amount of dust in the air. The ebru tray has just as much to say as the artist, or more, in the kind of ebru that is going to emerge.

• Copper

Copperware production is very old and that copper mines have long been operating in *Anatolia*. *Copper* is widely used in daily life for pots, jewelry, helmets, door-knockers, and to decorate doors. It is a widely used material in crafts. There are four techniques employed to make copperware. It is wrought, cast, plated or pressed.

a.

• Jewelry

The use of jewelry in *Anatolia* goes back to the *Neolithic* period. The *Hittites, Urartians, Lydians* and the *Phrygians*, etc. continued with the same tradition.

b.

Throughout history, people were buried with their personal belongings; men with their weapons, women with jewelry. This actually showed the common belief in reincarnation. Jewelry excavated in burial sites tells us a lot about jewelry production in those times. Contemporary artists often create new styles based on the designs of antique jewelry.

Anatolian women convey their messages, their expectations, and their status in society with the jewelry that they wear. It is, at the same time, an investment. When a baby is born, the people who come to congratulate the new mother will bring various pieces of jewelry, mostly gold coins with evil eyes. The husband will present some jewelry to the new mother.

Gifts of jewelry are given to a prospective bride at her engagement ceremony or to a bride at her wedding.

Gold and silver jewelry is produced by a variety of centuries-old techniques, such as filigree, relief, embossing, inlaying or using precious stones. All these beautiful modern and ancient jewelry pieces fill the windows of jewelers' shops. You may be overwhelmed by the abundance of jewelry and the variety of designs. Don't think that the designs are ordinary or common just because you see so many of them together. Take advantage of the fact that İstanbul is one of the finest gold centers in the world.

• *Glassware*

The traditional art of glassware in Turkey goes back to the *Seljuk* and the *Ottoman* periods. The traditional glass industry produced some of its finest products during the 17-18C. The *Ottoman* glass industry was located in and around İstanbul.

The first national glass factory was founded at *Paşabahçe* on the *Bosphorus* in 1934. The *Paşabahçe* glass factory gathered many glass craftsmen from all over the country. One of the traditional Turkish glassware techniques is *Çeşmibülbül* or Turkish filigree.

In addition to **Çeşmibülbül**, Turkish glassware appears to have used forms and styles suitable for applied and brushwork decoration, with a particular emphasis on designs inherited from the art of ceramics.

• *Meerschaum (Lületaşı)*

Meerschaum is actually a German word describing a soft mineral sometimes found floating on the *Black Sea*. It literally means *sea foam* alluding to the belief that it was the compressed whitecaps of waves, just as it is said in mythology to represent the goddess of beauty – *Aphrodite*. It has an opaque white or cream color and, is soft when first extracted. Meerschaum can be readily scratched with the nail. It gets harder when exposed to sun or dried in a warm room or in a furnace.

The city of **Eskişehir** in central Turkey has the purest and whitest, easiest to engrave *Meerschaum* in the world. It occurs in irregular nodular masses, in alluvial deposits, which are extensively worked for its extraction. It is said that in this district there are 4000 shafts leading to horizontal galleries for extraction of the meerschaum.

Nearly 300 years ago, the first meerschaum was carved by hand. Today artisans continue to create wonderful sculpture items and smoking pipes from this stone.

• *Leather*

Leather processing is a traditional handicraft in Turkey and was highly developed during the *Ottoman* period.

Although it is a big industry, the appeal for leather is still very dependent on personal appeal and touch. Leather processing is also risky, time-consuming, laborious and therefore costly. It takes about 45 days to transform a skin into leather ready for dying and nearly 60 days from skinning to the finished garment. The volume of livestock in Turkey is not increasing at a sufficiently high rate to keep up with the industry's demand. Despite all these difficulties, the leather sector is second only to textiles in terms of export figures. The principal markets for Turkish leather goods today are the European Union countries, led by Germany and then France.

When purchasing leather goods, one should be aware of the very wide range of products; different animal skins, baby lamb, lamb, suede, nubuk, pelluria, etc. and their differing qualities and prices.

a.

• **Textile**

Turkish fabrics are unique in weaving techniques, materials used, and designs reflecting Turkish culture. Hundreds of names, such as ***Kadife, Atlas, Gezi, Canfes, Selimiye, Hatayi, Çatma, Seraser, Sevayi***, etc., are used to identify various fabrics. The most commonly used material is silk with gold and silver threads, rich in motifs such as flowers (tulips, carnations, roses, spring blossoms, and hyacinths), trees (apple, date palm, cypress), animals (peacock, deer), crescent moon, star motifs, fruit (pomegranate, apple, date, artichoke, pineapple), etc.

- *Traditional & Modern Clothing*
- *Silk Scarves and Ties*
- *Pashmina Shawls*

b.

• Evil Eye Souvenirs

It is generally believed that children or beautiful people are vulnerable to evil eyes either because of jealousy or over affection. Therefore people attach an evil eye with *Maşallah* (God preserve) written on it on children's clothes or things to be protected against any kind of evil eyes. This eye is known as *nazar boncuğu* in Turkish and is made of a blue bead, as blue has a very effective impact, and acts as a charm to ward off evil influences from others.

In Turkey, wherever you look, you'll see plenty of evil eyes looking at you. People hang evil eye amulets in their cars and at the entrances to their houses or offices. It is customary to wear evil eyes in the form of jewelry; they come as bracelets, necklaces, anklets, gold or silver charms and pendants, talismans, and earrings, etc.

• Kilim Bags & Other Products

You can find a variety of high quality purses, bags, wallets, coasters or even shoes made out of fine leather and handmade old kilims.

• Spices

Lots of spices are used in *Turkish Cuisine*. Why do we use so many spices? Since eating is mankind's most fundamental need, we are looking for different tastes and different fragrances in our dishes. Spices were also needed in the preservation of food, such as the spicy paste coating the Turkish preserved meat known as *pastırma*.

Another reason for using spices is medicinal. Spices have been used to cure lots of diseases or prevent them. So, why not use them in our meals? See the Food section for a full list of spices and herbs in both Turkish and English.

• Apple Tea

The world's first instant hot apple drink is a sweetened powder to be mixed with hot water. It is served in traditional tulip-shaped tiny glasses. You can also buy it in the conventional form that is boiled before serving.

• Turkish Delight (Lokum)

Also called *Turkish Delight*, lokum is cubes of jelly-like or gummy confection flavored with flower or fruit essences, filled with various nuts, and dusted with powdered sugar.

< Turkish Delight

• Waterpipe (Nargile)

Nargile is a single or multi-stemmed (glass-based) water pipe device for smoking. It is very popular in Turkey. Nargile operates by water filtration and indirect heat. It can be used for smoking herbal fruits.

The waterpipe is smoked on a social basis, usually in a cafe with friends. İstanbul has many nargile cafes where the waterpipe is offered with non-alcoholic drinks (mainly tea or coffee).

People use nargile cafes to watch national sports games, popular TV shows, etc. and smoke the waterpipe to socialize.

• Chess Sets, Chess Boards and Backgammon Boards

Chess sets and boards made of onyx or wood are commonly available. Backgammon is a traditional game in Turkey. Very ornate backgammon boards with inlaid materials are on display in many stores.

• Arts

All private museums like Pera, Sabancı, Sadberk Hanım and İstanbul Modern have beautiful museum and art shops. İstanbul Modern has a museum and art shop also at the modern shopping mall of Kanyon.

- **Turkish Music CDs**

- *Homegrown* "İstanbul"
- *Mercan Dede* "Seyahatname"
- *Kudsi Ergüner* "Io"
- *Hilal Çalıkoğlu* "Turkish Classical Piano"
- *İstanbul Senfonisi* (Aşk, Boğaziçi, Düşler, Köprü, Saray, Doğu Rüzgarı)
- *Barbaros Erköse* "Cazname" (Instrumental Clarinet Music - Traditional)
- The London Academy of Ottoman Court Music *"European Music at the Ottoman Court"*
- *Hikmet Şimşek* "The Turkish Five" (Five best Turkish Composers – Classical Music)
- *Ahmed Adnan Saygun* "Yunus Emre Oratorio" (Conductor Hikmet Şimşek)
- *Burhan Öcal* "Kırklareli İl Sınırı" (Folk Music with hand-held drum and "zurna")
- *Okay Temiz* "Okay Temiz Klasikleri" (Instrumental Music with percussions and drums)

- **Turkish Movies & Documentaries**

- "Hittites" by *Tolga Örnek*
- "Troy - Ancient Myths and Unsolved Mysteries" by *National Geographic*

• *Turkish Books*

History

• "The Ottoman Empire: The Classical Age 1300-1600" by *Halil İnalcık*, Phoenix Press, London

• "Lords of the Horizons: A History of the Ottoman Empire" by *Jason Goodwin*

• "Ancient Turkey: A Travellers History of Anatolia" by *Seton Lloyd*

War History

• "Gallipoli: The Turkish Story" by *Kevin Fewster, Vecihi Basarin, Hatice Basarin,* Allen & Unwin

Culture-Travel

• "Turkish Odyssey: A Cultural Guide to Turkey" by *Şerif Yenen*

Novel

• All novels of *Orhan Pamuk*, (2006 Nobel Prize Winner)
• "The Other Side of the Mountain" by *Erendiz Atasü*, Milet Ltd, London

Poetry

• "The Illustrated Rumi: A Treasury of Wisdom from the Poet of the Soul" by *Jalalu'ddin Rumi*, Harper San Francisco

• "Poems of Nazim Hikmet", Revised and Expanded Edition by *Nazim Hikmet, Randy Blasing, Mutlu Konuk* Blasing- Persea Books

- **Turkish Books**

Cooking
- "Turkish Cooking" by *Gülseren Sancaklı and Margaret Oliphant*, A Yayınları

Children's Books
- "Nasrettin Hoca Jokes"
- "Zeynep, The Seagull of Galata Tower" by *Julia Townsend*, Çitlembik

WHERE TO BUY

- **Grand Bazaar**
See "If you have only one day in İstanbul" section in Highlights in İstanbul.

- **Egyptian (Spice) Bazaar**
See "If you have a second day in İstanbul" section in Highlights in İstanbul.

- **Balık Pazarı (Spices and Fish)**

İstiklal Caddesi
Çiçek Pasajı yanı

Fruits and Vegetables in the Balık Pazarı >

• *Ortaköy*

Ortaköy's open-air craft market is worth seeing at
the weekends.

• *Local Markets*

Almost every neighborhood in İstanbul has an open market on
a fixed day of the week. Stalls are filled with vegetables, fruits,
textiles, etc. Vendors yell, trying to sell their wares. There is a
great deal of bargaining.

The markets are known by the name of the neighborhood or
the name of the day on which it is set up.

For instance, *Wednesday Market* is in **Çarşamba-Fatih**, *Tuesday Market* is in **Kadıköy** or *Saturday Market* is in **Beşiktaş**.

• *Second-hand Book Bazaar (Sahaflar Çarşısı)*

Sahaflar Çarşısı is located between the *Grand Bazaar*'s Fes-
çiler *Gate* and the *Beyazit Mosque* in the *Bayezit Square*. It is
the oldest book bazaar dating back to the *Ottoman* times. It is
said that the book and paper market in the Byzantine period
was in the same location.

• *State-run Handicraft Stores*

DÖSİM

DÖSİM, run by the *Ministry of Culture and Tourism*, is a very
prestigious chain store selling fine representatives of authentic
handicrafts from the *Turkish Culture* among which, are kilims,
souvenirs made of wood, copper and glass, silver ornaments,
fabrics with Turkish motifs, etc.

Topkapı El Sanatları Mağazası

Topkapı Palace Museum,
First Courtyard, Next to the Ticket Office
212 - 513 3134

Bahçekapı El Sanatları Satış Mağazası

Şeyhülislam Hayri Efendi Cad.
No: 2/1, Bahçekapı-Eminönü
212 - 526 6813

• Çukurcuma

Located between Cihangir
and İstiklal Street, Çukurcuma
with its winding streets, is the
city's funky antiques district,
where you can get anything
from old musical istruments
to decorative items from
Turkish houses. With lots of
new galleries, cafes and design offices, Çukurcuma has
also become an art center.

Its graceful but decaying
early 20th-century buildings
are slowly getting face-lifts.
But the neighborhood, once
home to a large Greek community, has managed to keep
a balance between its original
flea market charm and new-
found galleries and designer
boutiques.

Horhor Antiques Bazaar

This is the largest antiques
bazaar in Turkey with more
than 200 shops on 6 floors.

Open Monday through
Saturday:
10:00 AM – 6:00 PM
Sunday: Noon – 5:00 PM

Horhor Cad.
Kırık Tulumba Sk. No: 13,
Fatih
212 - 523 6891
www.horhor.com

• Üsküdar Antiques Bazaar

It was formerly a flea market
but today with approximately
20 shops it has become a
nice, little antiques bazaar.

İnkılap Mah. Büyük Hamam
Sk. No: 18, Üsküdar

Khaftan Art & Antique

Nakilbend Sk. No: 33
Sultanahmet
212 - 458 5425
www.khaftan.com

Armaggan

Armaggan (Unique by
Design) produces unique
artistic objects, textiles and
jewelry in limited quantities.

Cumhuriyet Cad. 17/2 Taksim
212 - 297 71 00
www.armaggan.com

Günseli Kato Tasarım
Painting Artist Günseli Kato
has opened her art shop
at the Çırağan Palace
Kempinski Hotel.
Çırağan Caddesi No: 32,
Dükkan No: 13, Beşiktaş
212 - 227 3518
212 - 326 4646 ext. 7218

Hiref - Design Your Culture
İstinye Park Shopping Mall
İstinye
212 - 345 6038
www.hiref.com.tr

• *Shopping Centers (Malls)*
Cevahir
Büyükdere Cad. No: 22, Şişli
212 - 380 1352
www.istanbulcevahir.com

Profilo
Cemal Sahir Cad. No: 6-28,
Mecidiyeköy
212 - 216 4400
www.profiloalisverismerkezi.com.tr

Akmerkez
Nispetiye Cad.
Ulus / Etiler
212 - 282 0170
www.akmerkez.com.tr

Kanyon
Büyükdere Cad. No: 185,
Levent
212 - 353 5300
www.kanyon.com.tr

Metrocity
Büyükdere Cad., 1. Levent
212 - 344 0660
www.metrocity.com.tr

İstinye Park
İstinye Bayırı Cad. İstinye
212 - 345 5555

Capitol
Mahir İz Cad., Altunizade
216 - 554 7777
www.capitol.com.tr

Carousel
Halit Ziya Uşaklıgil Cad.
No: 1, Bakırköy
212 - 570 8434
www.carousel.com.tr

Baklava

• *Sweetshops*
Karaköy Güllüoğlu
Baklava Shop
Katlı Otopark Altı, Karaköy
www.gulluoglu.biz

Ali Muhittin Hacı Bekir
Hamidiye Cad. No: 83,
Eminönü
212 - 522 0666

İstiklal Cad. No: 127, Beyoğlu
212 - 244 2904

Koska (Chain Store)
www.koskahelvacisi.com.tr

Saray Muhallebicisi
(Chain Store)
www.saraymuhallebicisi.com

Kafkas Candied Chestnuts
(Chain Store)
www.kafkas.com.tr

Kahve Dünyası (Chain Store)
www.kahvedunyasi.com

TAX FREE SHOPPING IN TURKEY

In Turkey, there are many opportunities to
benefit from Tax Free Shopping, more than
2,000 retail outlets offer the service.
The affiliated stores display the Tax Free
Shopping logo.

You pay 18% or 8% VAT on the purchases
you make. The VAT is included in the price.
All visitors residing outside of Turkey, including *Turkish Nationals* living abroad are
entitled to claim back the tax, if they spend
100.00 TL + VAT (approx. US$90) or more in
one shop in one day.

The goods need to be exported within three months following
the month of purchase. After deduction of the handling
expense, you will receive a refund of up to 12.5% of the
15.25% of VAT included in the purchase price. You can cash
your refund check in Turkey or abroad at one of more than
200 international cash refund offices.

Global Refund offers you several possibilities of receiving
your VAT-refund:

    - Cash at a nearby Global Refund Office
    - Cash refund when you return home
    - Direct crediting of a chosen credit card or
      a local bank account in Turkey
    - Bank check sent to a chosen address

Entertainment
& Art

NIGHT CLUBS

• Folk & Belly Dancer Shows

Kervansaray Restaurant & Night Club
Cumhuriyet Cad.
No: 30, Harbiye
www.kervansaraygroup.com

Orient House İstanbul
Tiyatro Cad. No: 27, Beyazıt
212 - 517 6163
www.orienthouseistanbul.com

Biletix - Tickets for Events

Biletix, a subsidiary of Ticketmaster, is the first and largest entertainment ticketing company in Turkey. Serving more than 400 event organizers, sports teams, and venues each year, Biletix processes over 3.5 million tickets valued at over $60 million. *Biletix* sells tickets via web, one of Turkey's largest e-commerce websites, the *Biletix* call center, and via approximately 40 retail outlets located in major cities throughout the country.

Call Center: 216 - 556 9800
www.biletix.com

Ticket Turk - Tickets for Events

Ticket Turk is another ticketing company which has sold more than 2.5 million tickets of more than 7000 events within three years.

Call Center: 212 - 478 0600
www.ticketturk.com

< Belly Dancer

• Jazz, Rock or Pop Music

Babylon
Şeyhbender Sk. No: 3
Asmalımescit, Tünel
212 - 292 7368
www.babylon-ist.com

Balans
İstiklal Cad. Balo Sk.
No: 22, Beyoğlu
212 - 251 7020
www.balanstonique.com

**Ghetto - Genuine
Music Lounge**
Kalyoncu Kulluk Cad.
No: 10, Beyoğlu
212 - 251 7501
www.ghettoist.com

Hayal Kahvesi
Büyükparmakkapı Sk.
Afrika Han No: 19
Beyoğlu
212 - 244 2558
www.hayalkahvesibeyoglu.com

Indigo
Gümüşsuyu Mah.
Osmanlı Sk. Alara Han
No: 11/10, Taksim
212 - 244 8567
www.livingindigo.com

Nardis Jazz Club
Kuledibi Sk.
No: 14, Galata
212 - 244 6327
www.nardisjazz.com

Otto
Asmalımescit Mah.
Şeyhbender Sk.
No: 5, Beyoğlu
212 - 292 7015
www.otto-pgb.com

Reina
Muallim Naci Cad.
No: 10, Ortaköy
212 - 259 5919
www.reina.com.tr

Revan Pera
Evliya Çelebi Mah.
Refik Saydam Cad.
No: 15/A, Beyoğlu
212 - 243 6565
www.revan.com.tr

Riddim
Sıraselviler Cad.
No: 69/1, Taksim
212 - 251 2723
www.riddim.com.tr

< Reina Club

• *Soccer*

Turkish people are fanatic for soccer. Turks actually call it football. Fanaticism began in Turkey with the national soccer championships.

Taking the third place in the World Cup in 2002 and the third place in the European Cup in 2008, Turkish people even became more soccer fanatic.

The major soccer teams from Istanbul are Besiktas (black and white), Fenerbahçe (yellow and navy blue) and, Galatasaray (yellow and red).

These names are also district names in İstanbul. Each club has its own soccer stadium. Soccer players' transfer fees and salaries are incredibly high like in Europe.

Turkish soccer teams are bringing international players and coaches to play in their own teams. Some of them are Didi, Tafarel, Parreira, Ronaldo Guiaro, Cesar Prates and Marco Aurélio, etc.

Recently, popular Turkish players have been İlhan Mansız, Emre Belözoğlu, Bülent, Hakan Şükür (Turkish internationalist), Hasan, Nihat (Turkish internationalist playing in Spain), and goalkeeper Rüştü Rençber. Rüştü was one of the best goalkeepers at the World Cup 2002 and played in Spain for Barcelona.

One of the most outstanding achievements of Turkey in the field of sports is the UEFA Championship of Galatasaray in 2000. Having challenged by the most powerful soccer teams of Europe, and becoming qualified for the final without losing a single match, Galatasaray, in the final, defeated the British team Arsenal 4-1 and also became the first Turkish team to win the cup. Galatasaray also won the super cup against Real Madrid that same year. Galatasaray, which has so far had 138 matches in the European Cups, became Turkey's envoy to the west in soccer.

You should stay away from fanatics after derby matches among the top three teams,

namely Galatasaray, Fenerbahçe and Beşiktaş. They go
crazy and make lots of noise
in long convoys.

Turkish Football Federation
Konaklar Mah. Ihlamurlu Sk.
No: 9, 4. Levent
212 - 282 7020-8
www.tff.org
www.besiktas.org
www.fenerbahce.org
www.galatasaray.org

• *Basketball*

Basketball was introduced
to Turkey in 1904 by Ameri-
cans at the *Robert College*
in İstanbul. *Galatasaray High
School* formed the first basketball team in 1911. The next
basketball team was *Fenerbahçe* in 1913. An unofficial
league was founded in 1927
in İstanbul. A regional official
league was established in
1933. Basketball championships have been organized
among the leading clubs of
major cities like İstanbul, Ankara and İzmir since 1946.

The Turkish Basketball League
was founded in 1969 by

the *Turkish Basketball Fed-
eration*. Major teams from
İstanbul are *Fenerbahçe
Ülker*, *Galatasaray Café
Crown*, *Efes Pilsen S.K.* and
Beşiktaş Cola Turka.

Turkish Basketball Federation
Abdi İpekçi Spor Merkezi,
10. Yıl Cad, Zeytinburnu
212 - 679 7420
www.tbf.org.tr
www.fenerbahce.org
www.galatasaray.org
www.efesbasket.org
www.bjk.com.tr

• *Tennis*

İstanbul Cup (Third week of May)
İstanbul Cup is one of the
63 tournaments on the *Sony
Ericsson WTA*. It has been
organized since 2005. The
first tournament has attracted
attention from tennis authori-
ties and tennis lover's because of the show games and
matches. The tournament
champion *Venus Williams*
played an intercontinental
match with the Turkish tennis
player *İpek Şenoğlu* on the
Bosphorus Bridge.

Next page: Atatürk Olympic Stadium >>

This match was the first tennis match played between two continents.

212 - 438 0925
www.istanbulcup.com

Conrad Health Club

Conrad International İstanbul
Yıldız Cad. Beşiktaş
212 - 227 30 00
www.conradhotels1.hilton.com

Hillside City Club

Tepecik Yolu Alkent
Etiler
212 - 352 2333
www.hillside.com.tr

İstanbul Tennis Club

Poligon Mah. Aydınlar Cad.
No: 3/A, İstinye
212 - 229 1873,
212 - 229 1968
www.istanbulteniskulubu.org.tr

Raket Tennis Club

Ogün Sk. No: 17
Caddebostan
216 - 360 0115
www.raket.com

Swissotel The Bosphorus

Bayıldım Cad.
No: 2, Maçka
212 - 326 1100
www.swissotel.com.tr

• Golf

İstanbul Golf Club (9 holes)

Büyükdere Cad.
Harp Akademileri içi,
Eski Oto Sanayi Sitesi Karşısı,
Yeni Levent
212 - 324 0609
www.igk.org.tr

Klassis Golf and Country Club (18 Holes)

Seymen Köyü
Altıntepe Mevkii, Silivri
90 - 212 710 1300
www.klassisgolf.com.tr

Kemer Golf and Country Club (18 Holes)

Göktur Köyü
Uzun Kemer Mevkii,
Kemerburgaz
212 - 239 7010
www.kg-cc.com

• Skating

Galleria

Sahilyolu, Ataköy
212 - 559 9560
www.galleria-atakoy.com.tr

Florya Ice Park

Halkalı Cad. No: 63
Şenlikköy, Florya
212 - 579 1817

Parkorman
Maslak
212 - 328 2041
www.parkorman.com.tr

• *Bridge Clubs*

**İstanbul Bridge
Sports Club**
Yeniçeri Sk. Hedef İş hanı 2/2
Emniyet Evleri, 4. Levent
212 - 283 8757 - 59
www.istanbulbric.com

Kadıköy Bridge Club
Bağdat Cad. Orkide Apt.
No: 81/1, Kızıltoprak
216 - 336 4539
www.kadikoybric.com

**Majör Boğaziçi Bridge
Sports Club**
Yanarsu Sk. M. Çelik Apt.
No: 58/1, Etiler
212 - 351 0676
212 - 351 6323
www.majorbogazici.com

• *Chess Clubs*

**İstanbul Chess
Training Center**
Levazım Sitesi Blok: H5
D: 24, Levent
532 - 421 0799
www.istanbulsatranc.net

İstanbul Chess Center
Perpa 11. Kat B Blok
No: 1568, Okmeydanı
www.satrancmerkezi.com

Turkish Chess Federation
312 - 309 7594
www.tsf.org.tr

• *Equestrian Clubs*

İstanbul Equestrian Club
Maslak Üçyol Mevkii,
Binicilik Tesisleri, Maslak
212 - 276 2056
212 - 286 3840
www.istanbulatlisporkulubu.com

**S International
Equestrian Center**
S Uluslararası Binicilik Merkezi
İstinye Yokuşu, Tepeüstü Sk.
No: 1, İstinye
212 - 323 2100
www.sbinicilik.com

**Turkish Equestrian
Federation**
Uzun Kemer Mevkii
Göktürk Belediyesi, Eyüp
212 - 239 7038
212 - 239 8736
www.binicilik.org.tr

• Sailing Clubs

İstanbul Sailing Academy
Münir Nurettin Selçuk Cad.
No: 26/1, Kalamış
216 - 449 9560
www.istsailing.com

İstanbul Sailing Club
Fenerbahçe Burnu
Kadiköy
216 - 336 0633
www.istanbulyelken.org.tr

Kalamış Sailing Club
Kalamış Fener Cad.
İskele Sk. No: 2
Kalamış, Kadıköy
www.kalamisyelken.org

• Diving

Ayışığı Diving Center
Biber Turizm
Bağdat Cad. İclaliye Apt.
No: 24/4
Kızıltoprak, Kadıköy
216 - 349 5689
www.ayisigidiving.com

Balıkadamlar Spor Kulübü
İskele Çıkmazı No: 69
Caddebostan, Kadıköy
216 - 355 5628
www.bsk.org.tr

Bubble Club
Başa Sk. Oral Apt.
No: 12/2 , 1. Levent
212 - 264 5774
212 - 264 5627
www.divebubbleclub.com

• İstanbul Eurasia Marathon

(Third or fourth Sunday of October)

The 15-kilometer (10-mile) *İstanbul Eurasia Marathon* starts from the Asian side of İstanbul and ends at the European side while taking the runners to the most beautiful spots in town.

The Metropolitan Municipality of İstanbul organizes the marathon.

Neslişah Mah. Kaleboyu Cad.
No: 11, Fatih
212 - 453 3000
www.istanbulmarathon.org

• Formula 1 Grand Prix İstanbul

(Second weekend of May)

The *Formula 1 Grand Prix İstanbul* site is located on the Asian side of İstanbul, close to the newly constructed *Sabiha Gökçen İstanbul Airport*. In addition to easy access from TEM (Trans European Motorway) and the airport, the grounds are located within the green belt surrounded by forest and cultivated green fields.

The total area allocated for the İstanbul *Park Circuit* is 2,215,000 square meters. The track that runs anti-clockwise is 5,333 meter (3313 miles) long. The circuit is composed of 14 curves, of which six are right turns and eight left turns.

216 - 677 1010
www.formula1-istanbul.com

(Second and third weeks of June)

• *Red Bull Air Race*

The *Red Bull Air Race World Series* features the world's best pilots in a motor sports competition based on speed, precision and skill. It has taken place above the *Golden Horn* in İstanbul since 2006.
www.redbullairrace.com

NEAREST BEACHES

• *Kilyos*

Dalia Beach Club
Kilyos Yolu Dalyan Mevkii
Demirciköy, Sarıyer
212 - 204 0368
212 - 204 0169
www.clubdalia.com

Golden Beach Club
Marmaracık Koyu
Rumelifeneri
212 - 325 5583
www.goldenbeachclub.net

Non-Stop Beach
Kilyos Turban Yolu
No: 4, Kilyos
212 - 219 2293
www.nonstopbeach.com

Seanergy Beach Club
Gümüşdere
Kumluk Mevkii, Kilyos
212 - 203 0863
www.seanergy.com

Solar Beach
Turban Yolu Cad.
No.4, Kilyos
212 - 201 2139
www.solarbeach.net

• Şile & Ağva

Şile and *Ağva* have nice long sandy beaches on the *Black Sea* coast, northeast of the *Anatolian* side. Bus service and fast sea buses are available on weekends.

Famous beaches are; *Ağlayan Kaya, Kumbaba, Ayaza, İmrenli, Sahilköy, Ağva* and *Kurfallı*.

• Princes' Islands

Yörükali Beach
Büyükada
216 - 382 7341
216 - 382 7394
www.yorukali.com

Sadıkbey Beach
Halki Palace
Heybeliada
216 - 351 0025
www.halkipalacehotel.com

Kalpazankaya
Burgazada
216 - 381 1504
www.kalpazankaya.com

Kamos Beach Club
Ayazma, Kınalıada
216 - 381 6913 / 381 6195

• Other Beaches

True Blue
Fener Kalamış Cad.
Marina Karşısı
Fenerbahçe
216 - 550 5195
www.truebluebeach.com

Dodo İstanbul Sea Club
Mercan Çınarlı Sk.
No: 1, Tuzla
216 - 446 8737
www.dodoistanbul.com

**Wattabe
Experience Center**
Alkent 2000 Lakeside
Büyükçekmece
212 - 857 8292
www.wattabe.com.tr

MUSIC

Atatürk Cultural Center – AKM (Opera House)

İstanbul State Opera and Ballet has frequent performances at AKM October through May. It is located right at the Taksim Square and has two multi-purpose halls, one with 1300 and the other 500 seat capacities.

Atatürk Kültür Merkezi
Taksim, 212 - 251 5600
www.idobale.com

Cemal Reşit Rey (CRR) Concert Hall

This concert hall was named after Turkish composer *Cemal Reşit Rey* and is operated and subsidised by İstanbul Metropolitan Municipality. Its main hall has a seating capacity of 850 people.

Activities held here have a wide range from *London Royal Philharmonic Orchestra* or *Turkish Classical Music* to *Blues* or *Turkish Folk*.

Darülbedayi Cad. Harbiye
212 - 232 9830
212 - 240 5012
www.crrks.org

Garaj İstanbul

The *Garaj İstanbul* Project is a journey that started with the rental of the *Galatasaray* Car Park in 2005, in order to create an "empty space" where the creations of "today" and "now" could gain visibility in Turkey's contemporary scene of theater, dance, music, and other interdisciplinary arts.

This idea was shared with artists, friends, interested groups, and business people. Today it has become Turkey's *Civic Cultural Transformation Project*, and is one of the most renowned cultural centers in Europe.

Tomtom Mah. Yeni Çarşı Cad. Kaymakam Reşat Bey Sk. No: 11/A, Galatasaray
Beyoğlu
212 - 244 4499
www.garajistanbul.com

İş Sanat Arts and Culture Centre

İş Sanat, located in the İş Towers, opened its doors on November 4, 2000 with a performance by the *Royal Philharmonic Orchestra*.

Next page: Symphony Orchestra, Cemal Reşit Rey Concert Hall >>

So far over 250,000 people have attended the events of *İş Sanat*. In addition to select performances of classical music, jazz, traditional Turkish music and world music, dance performances, plays, and poetry readings are staged at the 800 seat *İstanbul Hall of İş Sanat Arts and Culture Centre*.

İş Kuleleri, Levent
212 - 316 1083
www.issanat.com.tr

Akbank Art Center

Founded in 1992, *Akbank Chamber Orchestra* is one of the first examples of music supported by the private sector. The orchestra has a very special place in the realm of classical music in Turkey and is characterized by its dynamic programming and by the quality of its performances.

The *Akbank Chamber Orchestra* has performed almost 25 concerts each year, including regular concert series on two sides of İstanbul. The *Anatolian* tours and *Youth*

Concerts are usually set at different universities.

İstiklal Cad. Zambak Sk. No: 1, Beyoğlu
212 - 252 3500
www.akbanksanat.com

Babylon

With a capacity that can accommodate 450 standing or 350 tables plus standing, the Babylon opened in 1999 with a concert by *John Lurie & the Lounge Lizards*. Over the past years the venue has hosted hundreds of bands and has staged over 1500 concerts.

Şeyhbender Sk. No: 3, Tünel Asmalımescit, Beyoğlu
212 - 292 73 68
www.babylon-ist.com

Borusan Philharmonic Orchestra

The Borusan Culture and Arts (BKS) Center, founded in 1997, presents various cultural projects. *The Borusan Philharmonic Orchestra (BIFO)*, led by *Permanent Maestro Gürer Aykal*, began performing a couple of years before the founding of BKS, and became its backbone. In addition to the activities in the area of classical music, the *Borusan* has created an extensive musical library.

Borusan Kültür ve Sanat
İstiklal Cad. No: 213, Beyoğlu
212 - 336 3280
www.borusansanat.com

Turkcell Kuruçeşme Arena

Turkcell Kuruçeşme Arena is a multi purpose concert and entertainment venue located on a 10.000 m² open space on the *Ortaköy-Arnavutköy* strip of the *Bosphorus*.

Among those musicians who have given concerts there are: *Shakira, Stomp, Sting, Roger Waters, and Depeche Mode.*

Muallim Naci Cad.
No: 60, Kuruçeşme
www.kurucesmearena.net

FESTIVALS

International İstanbul Film Festival (April)

The International İstanbul Film Festival was inaugurated as a film week in 1982, as part of the *International İstanbul Festival*. Beginning in 1984, the event became a separate activity and was shifted to April. In 1985, two competitive sections, one national and the other international, were included in the *Festival* program. Accredited by FIAPF since 1989, the Festival features a thematically specialized international competition, provides a showcase for recent Turkish film productions, and thus represents a rewarding medium where Turkish and foreign filmmakers get together. The *Festival* draws special interest to world classics, presenting retrospective sections within its programs, particularly attended by young audiences.

İstanbul Foundation for Culture and Arts
212 - 334 0700
www.iksv.org

International İstanbul Theater Festival (Third week of May through the first week of June)

The International İstanbul Theater Festival, a biennial

since 2001, was first held in 1989. The Festival presents the finest examples of Turkish theater as well as internationally acclaimed theater companies and dance groups. Carefully selected companies and artists who participate in the *Festival* stimulate the world theater scene with their impressive and, at times, radical creations. Whether modern or post-modern, various impressive forms of contemporary theater come within the scope of the International *İstanbul Theater Festival*.

İstanbul Foundation for Culture and Arts
212 - 334 0700
www.iksv.org

International İstanbul Music Festival (June)

The first *International İstanbul Music Festival*, the flagship of the International İstanbul Festivals, took place in 1973 originally under the title İstanbul *Festival*. From its inception it has included in its programs the finest examples of artistic creativity in the fields of classical music, classical ballet and contemporary dance, opera, folklore, jazz/pop, cinema, drama and visual arts from both Turkey and abroad, as well as seminars, conferences and lectures. In 1986, the Film and then the Theater, Jazz festivals and the Biennial separated as distinct events, and the name of the International *İstanbul Festival* was changed to International *İstanbul Music Festival* in 1994. Since then the Festival especially emphasises "sharing artistic inspiration" and creates programs in which international orchestras and conductors perform with Turkish soloists or vice versa.

İstanbul Foundation for Culture and Arts
212 - 334 0700
www.iksv.org

International İstanbul Jazz Festival

(First three weeks of July)

From the beginning, the *Festival* was meant to go beyond the limits of "jazz" and its

literal meaning. It was to embrace many other styles in addition to jazz: rock, pop, blues, reggae, new age and more.

It would surpass the bound-aries of the concert venues and question the borders separating the artists from the audience. In short, it would be more than a series of concerts. The result has been eleven years of success with over 300 concerts by thousands of performers in numerous venues, clubs and even the streets and squares of İstanbul. A jubilant fes-tival takes place in the very heart of the city. One of the best-organ-ized festivals in Europe, the *International İstanbul Jazz Festival* has brought many renowned artists.

İstanbul Foundation for
Culture and Arts
212 - 334 0700
www.iksv.org

International İstanbul Dance Festival

(First week of June)

Dance has become increasingly popular in Turkey, and this festival was initiated as a means of bring-ing together our modern dancers.

"İstanbuldans" is the name of the festival that embraces all dance performances staged at garaj istanbul within a brand new format that includes 'all' of dance.

Garaj İstanbul
Tomtom Mah. Yeni Çarşı Cad. Kaymakam Reşat Bey Sk.
No: 11/A, Galatasaray
Beyoğlu
212 - 244 4499
www.istanbuldancefest.com

International İstanbul Biennial

(Third week of September through the second week of November)

The International İstanbul Biennial was organised in 1987. The Biennial aims to create a meeting point in İstanbul in the field of visual arts between artists from diverse cultures and the

audience. The nine biennials have enabled the formation

of an international cultural network between local and international art circles, by bringing together new trends in contemporary art every two years.

Considered one of the most prestigious biennials, on a par with Venice, Sao Paolo and Sydney, the *International İstanbul Biennial* prefers an exhibition model that enables a dialogue between artists and the audience through the work of the artists instead of a national representation model. The curator, appointed by an international advisory board, develops the criteria by which a variety of artists and projects are invited to the exhibition.

İstanbul Foundation for Culture and Arts
212 - 334 0700
www.iksv.org

Rock'n Coke İstanbul

(First weekend of September)

UNDP and Coca-Cola Youth Fund aim to support projects that address the youth of Turkey in particular. The main interest area of the projects will be "raising standards of life" which is part of national sustainable development and progress plans and which are the priorities of UNDP.

Hezarfen Havalimanı
Çatalca
0800 261 1920
www.rockncoke.com

Efes Pilsen Blues Festival

(First week of November through the second week of December)

This started with two concerts in 1990. At present it has reached 270 thousand music lovers in various cities of Turkey. It brings together many notable musicians from all over the world.

Esentepe Mah. Anadolu Cad. No: 3 Kartal
216 - 444 3337
www.efesblues.com

Efes Pilsen One Love Festival

(Third weekend of June)

Since 2002 the *Efes Pilsen One Love Festival* has hosted notable musicians such as *Manu Chao-Gotan Project-Moby, Peter Gabriel, Chemical Brothers, and the Beastie Boys.*
Esentepe Mah. Anadolu Cad. No: 3 Kartal
444 3337
www.efespilsen.com.tr
www.efespilsenonelove.com

Contemporary İstanbul Art Festival

(Third and fourth weeks of December)

Contemporary İstanbul is an international contemporary art exhibition where national and international galleries selected by the *Contemporary İstanbul* Jury participate, and contemporary art is shown.

Mete Cad. No: 10, D: 11, Taksim
212 - 244 7171
www.contemporaryistanbul.com

İstanbul Design Week

(Second week of October)

İstanbul Design Week is a creativity platform presenting reference points for designers to draw their path. It is a connection point for creative ideas from different disciplines of design.

It aims at making İstanbul a meeting point for Turkish designers and the international design world by events, exhibits, panels, conferences and competitions all over the city.

Its unique venue, the Old Galata Bridge, differentiates *İstanbul Design Week* from similar design events. The century-old bridge is one of İstanbul's most important landmarks and used as the main exhibition area of *İstanbul Design Week*. Promising an extraordinary experience, the *Old Galata Bridge* has a total exhibit area of 10,000 square meters, a perfectly central location and a very unique atmosphere.

Meşrutiyet Cad.
Tarhan Han No: 99, Beyoğlu
212 - 252 6489
www.istanbuldesignweek.com

International İstanbul Tulip Festival

(Second week of April)

Tulips were introduced to Holland from *Anatolia* by *Ogier Ghiselin de Busbecq*. He was ambassador of *Charles V* to *Süleyman the Magnificen*t in 1554.

Tulips in İstanbul were very popular in the Ottoman times. There is even a period called the Tulip Period (1718-1730). All palaces and gardens were decorated with beautiful tulips.

In order to revive tulips again, the Metropolitan Municipality of İstanbul has been organizing this international festival since 2006. It takes place at the beginning of April and it includes many other cultural activities like exhibitions, performances, contests, etc.

212 - 455 1300
www.istanbulunlalesi.com

Ahırkapı *Hıdrellez* Festival

(Evening of May 5)

Hıdrellez is a festival to celebrate the first day of "early summer" in the whole Turkish World. *Hıdrellez Day* falls on May 5-6.

Legend has it that, *Hızır* is a prophet who has attained immortality and reached *God* by drinking the water of life, and wanders around among people from time to time, especially in the spring, and helps people who are in difficulty and distributes plenty and health.

a. Tulips

With the efforts and successful organization of the *Armada Hotel*, *Hıdrellez* has turned out to be an event with collective civil community participation. Each year the activities begin on *Ahırkapı Street* and spread to the adjacent streets. Towards midnight, people will start jumping over the traditional fires and individual wishes will be written on pieces of paper and attached on a "wish-tree".

b. Ahırkapı Hıdrellez Festival

A lot of spring food and drinks, local musicians' gypsy and Balkan music, street concerts and lots of people dancing in the street; this is what *Ahırkapı Hıdrellez Festival* is all about.

Ahırkapı Cad.
Cankurtaran, Sultanahmet
212 - 455 4455
(Armada Hotel)
www.hidrellez.org

AUCTI

ART GALLERIES & EXHIBITIONS

Alif Ar

Mim Ke

No: 17,

212 - 2

www.a

Antik I

Talimye

Maçka

212 - 2:

www.a

Artı M

Ahmet

No: 146

212 - 2:

www.a

Denizle

Cumhu

Elmada

212 - 36

www.de

Aksanat Art Gallery
İstiklal Cad. Zambak Sk.
No: 1,Beyoğlu
212 252 3500
www.akbanksanat.com

Almelek Art Gallery
Cevdet Paşa Cad. No: 99/1
Ayşe Sultan Korusu, Bebek
212 - 265 38 51
www.almelekartgallery.com

Artisan Art Gallery
Müfide Küley Sk.
(Poyracık Sk.)
No: 32/1, Nişantaşı
212 - 247 90 81
www.lebriz.com/v3_galleries

Borusan Art Gallery
İstiklal Cad. No: 421
Tünel, Beyoğlu
212 - 248 3165
www.borusansanat.com

dem-art Art Gallery
Sahilyolu Engin Apt.
No: 79/B, Arnavutköy
212 - 287 7867
www.dem-art.net

Doku Art Gallery
Av.Süreyya Ağaoğlu Sk.
No: 4/2, Teşvikiye
212 - 246 2496
www.dokusanat.com

Evin Art Gallery
Bebek deresi Sk.
No: 13, Bebek
212 - 265 8158
www.evin-art.com

Galata Photography House
Serdar-ı Ekrem Sk
No: 5, Galata
212 - 243 7187
www.galatafotografhanesi.com

Gallery Artist
Ayazma Cad.
No: 4, Fulya
212 - 227 6852
www.galeriartist.com

Gallery Nev
Maçka Cad. No: 33
Maçka
212 - 231 6763
www.galerinev.com

Hobi
Valiko
Nişant
212 - 2
www.

İFSAK
Exhib
İstiklal
No: 34
212 - 2
www.

İstanb
Photo
Tarlaba
Beyoğ
212 - 2
www.is

İş San
İş Kule
212 - 3
www.i

Kasa
Bankal
No: 2,
212 - 2
www.ka

Milli R
Teşvikiy
Teşvikiy
212 - 2
www.m

CONVENTION & EXHIBITION VENUES

İstanbul Convention and Visitors Bureau - ICVB

The İstanbul Convention and Visitors Bureau (ICVB), which was founded in 1997, is a non-profit, non-aligned marketing body and information-clearing house. It is dedicated to building İstanbul's potential as a destination and assisting companies and associations in getting the most out of their events in İstanbul. Working in close coordination with its members and other tourism industry associations, ICVB designs and implements strategic marketing campaigns and special events designed to raise Istanbul's profile as a conference and incentive destination.

ICVB provides information on the latest facilities and venues, conferences held or scheduled to be held in İstanbul, accommodation information, meeting planners' guide, coordination of inspection visits, press releases, general information about İstanbul, organization of international conferences and travel trade fairs for the local parties in the sector and many others.

Among ICVB's members are hotels, conference and exhibition centers, DMCs or PCOs, airlines and other companies involved in the conference and incentive tourism business.

ICVB
Halaskargazi Cad.
No: 297/5, Şişli
212 - 343 0000
www.icvb.org

Lütfi Kırdar - İstanbul Convention & Exhibition Center (ICEC)

The İstanbul Convention & Exhibition Center (ICEC) has everything you need to organize successful meetings and exhibitions in the city of İstanbul. The only place in İstanbul where 3,500 delegates can sit down together for a five-star gala dinner, ICEC offers you an outstanding combination of state-of-the-art facilities and superior service.

Cumhuriyet Cad.
Harbiye
212 - 373 1100
www.icec.org

Sütlüce Congress and Cultural Center

Sütlüce Congress and Cultural Center stands on the shores of the Golden Horn, an area of great historic interest. In addition to the 5 auditoriums with capacities ranging from 3000 to 275 people, it also has 9 meeting rooms with capacities of 150-60 people.

CNR EXPO Exhibition Center

CNR was founded as a Trade Fair Organizer in 1985 and has continued to grow since then. In addition to the fair organizer companies, service companies within CNR provide service to exhibitors and visitors for all their particular professional needs.

Atatürk Havalimanı Karşısı
Yeşilköy
212 - 665 7474
www.cnrexpo.com

İstanbul Hilton Convention & Exhibition Center

The Hilton İstanbul Hotel is the only international hotel in the city with its own convention center that can accommodate 3000 guests with 8 meeting rooms, a business center and an executive lounge.

Cumhuriyet Cad.
Harbiye
212 - 315 6000
www.istanbul.hilton.com

TÜYAP Fair Convention and Congress Center

Tüyap was established in 1979. The prevalent need for a modern exhibition center in the long term was met by the construction of "Tüyap Beylikdüzü Exhibition and Congress Center" in 1996.

This facility is the largest private exhibition center in Turkey.

E5 Karayolu Gürpınar Kavşağı
Beylikdüzü, Büyükçekmece
212 - 886 6886
www.tuyap.com.tr

World Trade Center İstanbul

World Trade Center İstanbul hosts 80 exhibitions annually at its large fairgrounds. Offering new markets and opportunities to thousands of companies, attracting hundreds of thousands of visitors, the fairgrounds are very important in the industry.

Atatürk Havalimanı Karşısı
Yeşilköy
212 - 465 6707
www.wtcistanbul.net

Grand Cevahir Hotel Convention Center

Darülaceze Cad.
No: 9, Şişli
212 - 314 4242
www.grandcevahirhotel.com

Military Museum Cultural Center

Harbiye
212 - 224 9600

Abdi İpekçi Arena

10. Yıl Cad.
Zeytinburnu
212 - 679 7420
www.tbf.org.tr

İstanbul Expo Center

Atatürk Havalimanı Karşısı
Yeşilköy
212 - 465 0303
www.wtcistanbul.net

Next page: Tuğra Restaurant Terrace, Çırağan Palace Kempinski Hotel >>

Food & Drinks

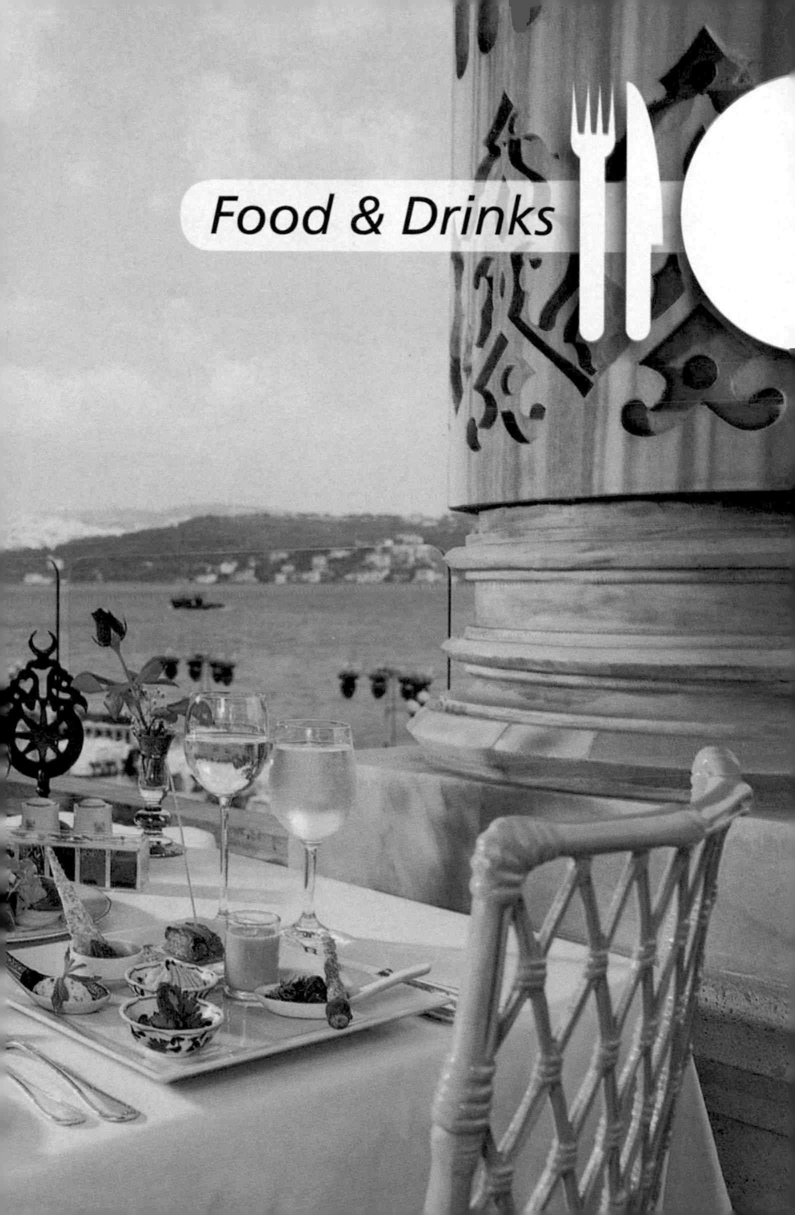

Turkish Cuisine is considered to be among the best in the world. So many civilizations, so many styles, and the abundant food supply contribute to today's cuisine.

"Afiyet olsun!" is an expression used to wish that a meal be enjoyed. Unlike other cultures, the expression is used both before and after the meal.

When anybody wants to express appreciation about food prepared by somebody else, he says *"Elinize sağlık!"* which means "May God give health to your hands". When proposing a toast, the expression *"Şerefe!"* is used which literally means "to your honor!"

LOKANTA

This kind of restaurant is typically Turkish and offers home-cooking style food. From a selection of meals, it is possible to go to the window and choose whatever you like.

Güveç is any kind of meat prepared in a casserole.

Bulgur Pilavı is cooked pounded wheat.

Dolma is stuffed vegetables, usually grape leaves, peppers, eggplants, cabbage leaves or mussels filled with rice, minced meat and raisins.

Hünkar Beğendi is *Sultan*'s delight. It is simply chopped lamb pieces served on eggplant puree.

Musakka is a very common eggplant dish with ground meat.

Karnıyarık is stuffed eggplant.

Meatballs, vegetables or liver are among traditional Turkish food. Offal; nothing is wasted; on the contrary, offal plays an important role in the *Turkish Cuisine*. Tripe, head, trotter, brain, tongue, intestine and liver are among the most common.

SPICES

Spices play a very important role in the *Turkish Cuisine*.
Here is a list of common spices and herbs:

adaçayı	sage	*kırmızı toz biber*	paprika
anason	aniseed	*kişniş otu*	coriander
biberiye	rosemary	*kuş burnu*	rose hip
çörekotu	black cumin	*mercanköşk*	marjoram
çöven	soapwort	*nane*	mint
defne	bay leaf	*roka*	rocket leaf
dereotu tohumu	dill	*safran*	saffron
hardal	mustard	*salep*	orchis
Hindistan cevizi	nutmeg	*sumak*	sumach
ıhlamur	linden	*tarçın*	cinnamon
karanfil	clove	*tere*	cress
kekik	thyme	*vanilya*	vanilla
kimyon	cumin	*yeni bahar*	allspice
kına	henna	*zencefil*	ginger
kırmızı biber	red pepper		

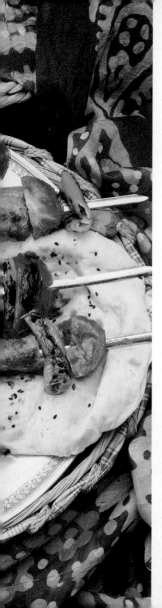

KEBAPÇI

This is the place where *kebap*s are sold. *Kebap* is roasted, broiled or grilled meat prepared in many different ways, each of them named by adding a word to *kebap*; *döner kebap, şiş kebap, patlıcan kebap*, etc.

Şiş Kebap is cubes of marinated chicken or lamb meat on skewers. Meat on skewers is grilled in a barbecue.

Adana Kebap is barbecued spicy meat mounted on a wide skewer This is ground lamb meat that is mixed with fat from lamb's tail.

Urfa Kebap is very similar but it is not spicy.

Köfte is grilled or fried meatballs.

Döner Kebap is lamb meat roasted on a revolving spit.

FARINACEOUS FOOD RESTAURANTS

These differ from Italian pizza to Turkish farinaceous foods such as *börekçi, pideci, lahmacuncu, mantıcı, simitçi*, etc.

Börek is layers of pastry filled with cheese, eggs, vegetables, or minced meat, then fried or baked.

Gözleme is very common in rural areas; it is thin dough (phyllo dough) filled with cheese and parsley or anything you like, and baked on a thin iron plate placed in a wood or charcoal fire.

a. Pide

Pide is a thick dough base filled or covered with any combination of meat, cheese, mushroom, eggs, etc. It is quite similar to pizza but served with butter and grated cheese.

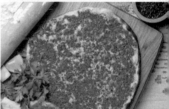
b. Lahmacun

Lahmacun is a thin round dough base covered with a spicy mixture of minced lamb meat, onions, tomatoes and parsley.

Mantı is a kind of pasta filled with minced lamb and served with yogurt, garlic and butter on top. *Mantı* is usually eaten as a main dish.

c. Simit

Simit is a circular crisp bread covered with sesame seeds, and is very common in Turkey. *Simit* is generally eaten plain, or for breakfast with cheese and tea. It is often sold by street vendors from pushcarts, or it is carried on a tray that they put on their heads.

MEYHANE & FISH RESTAURANTS

These restaurants serve proper dinners. First, a large variety of *soğuk* (cold) *meze*, (hors d'oeuvres or cold appetizers) are offered on a big tray from which you can choose a few, then you should sample a few *sıcak* (hot) *meze* before the main dish. The main dish will be either fish or meat. After having dessert or fruit, as the locals do, it is time to drink a cup of Turkish coffee.

Meze

Yoghurt is very important in *Turkish Cuisine*. The word yoghurt or yogurt is derived from the Turkish word *yoğurt*. It comes plain or with garlic. Many of the *mezes* are served with yoghurt.

Pilaki is beans cooked with garlic, tomato paste, carrot and olive oil.

Cacık is yoghurt with garlic, grated cucumber, dried mint and just a few drops of olive oil.

Dolma is stuffed vine leaves, cabbage leaves, chard, peppers, zuccini or eggplant. If it is made with olive oil and no meat, then it is a *meze*.

Arnavut Ciğeri meaning Albanian liver is fried liver. It is served with onions and parsley.

Fava is mashed broad beans.

Çerkez Tavuğu meaning Circassian chicken is poached chicken with walnut sauce.

< Dolma

Humus is mashed chickpeas with sesame, garlic, olive oil, and lemon juice.

Haydari is thick yogurt with garlic spread.

Köz Biber is barbecued red peppers with garlic and vinegar.

Acılı Ezme is hot spicy freshly mashed tomato spread with onion and green herbs.

Kısır is prepared with bulgur (pounded wheat), tomato paste, parsley, onion, garlic, sour pomegranate juice and lots of spices.

Piyaz is bean salad with onions and tomatoes.

Patlıcan Salatası is eggplant salad and is served in various ways. Barbecued eggplant is mashed and served with olive oil and parsley. Barbecued eggplant is chopped and mixed with onions, garlic, tomatos and parsley. It is also served with yoghurt.

Babaganuş is a kind of eggplant salad also.

Şakşuka is fried eggplant with tomato souce.

Çoban Salatası is shepherd's salad and it contains chopped tomatoes, peppers, and cucumbers with olive oil.

Roka Salatası is rocket leaf salad.

*Sıcak meze*s are served before the main course. Among them are fried mussels or squid, shrimp, various kinds of *börek*, fried potatoes, etc.

Stuffed Mussels >

Fish & Sea Products

Ahtapot	Octopus
Alabalık	Trout
Barbunya (Mullus barbatus)	Red Mullet
Çinekop	Younger Blue Fish (smaller than Sarıkanat)
Çipura (Sparus aurata)	Gilthead Sea Bream
Çiroz	Dried Mackerel
Deniz Kestanesi	Sea urchins
Dil Balığı (Solea solea)	Sole
Fener (Lophius piscatorius)	Angler
Gümüş Balığı (Atherina presbyter)	Sand Smelt
Hamsi (Engraulis encrasicolus)	European Anchovy
Havyar	Caviar
İskorpit, Lipsos (Scorpaena porcus)	Scorpion fish
İstakoz	Lobster
İstavrit (Scomber trachurus)	(Mediterranean) Horse Mackerel
İstiridye	Oyster
İzmarit (Spicara smaris)	Picarel
Kalamar	Squid
Kalkan (Rhombus maximus)	Turbot
Karagöz (Sargus rodeleti)	Sea Bream (black)
Karides	Shrimp
Kefal (Mugil cephalus)	Flathead Mullet
Kerevit	Crawfish
Kılıç (Xiphias gladius)	Swordfish
Kırlangıç (Trigla hirundo)	Tub Gurnard
Kofana	Larger Blue Fish
Kolyoz	Spanish Mackerel

Levrek (Dicentrarchus labrax)	Sea Bass
Lüfer (Pomatomus saltator)	Blue Fish
Mercan (Pagellus erythrinus)	Pandora
Mersin Balığı (Acipenser sturio)	Sturgeon
Mezgit (Merlangius merlangus)	Whiting (Chicken Fish)
Midye	Mussel
Orfoz (Epinephelus guazza)	Grouper
Palamut (Sarda sarda)	Bonito, Atlantic Bonito
Sardalya (Clupea sardina)	Sardine
Sarıkanat	Younger Blue Fish
Sazan (Cyprinus carpio)	Carp
Sinarit (Dentex dentex)	Dentex
Somon Balığı	Salmon
Ton, Orkinos (Thunnus thynnus)	Tuna Fish, Tunny
Turna (Sphyraena sphyraena)	Barracuda
Uskumru (Scomber scombrus)	Mackerel (Atlantic Mackerel)
Yayın Balığı	Pike
Yengeç	Crab
Zargana (Belone vulgaris)	Garfish

TATLICI

This is a place where they sell different kinds of sweets. There are many of them like *baklavacı, muhallebici, dondurmacı, helvacı*, etc.

Baklava

It is thin layers of flaky pastry stuffed with almond paste, walnuts or pistachio nuts in syrup. Its name comes from the shape in which it is cut; lozenge-shapes.

Kadayıf & Künefe

Kadayıf is shredded wheat in syrup. Künefe differs from Kadayıf with cheese in it. It is served hot.

Dough-based desserts

Dough-based desserts are *Ekmek Kadayıfı, Revani* (with semolina and starch), *Şekerpare, Kalburabasma, Dilber Dudağı, Vezir Parmağı, Hanım Göbeği, Kemalpaşa* and *Tulumba*. They are all served with syrup.

Aşure

Also called Noah's pudding, it is made from numerous (some 40) types of dried fruits and pulses.

Kaymak

Kaymak is thick clotted cream eaten with most sweets as well as on its own with honey or jam.

Sütlaç

This is rice pudding.

Kestane Şekeri

This sweet is glacé chestnuts (candied chestnuts). They are generally canned or kept in glass jars in syrup. The city of *Bursa* is famous with its **kestane şekeri**.

Pişmaniye

This is a sweet-meat made of sugar, flour and butter which resembles flax fibers.

Tahin-Pekmez

It is a mixture of both tahin (sesame oil) and pekmez (molasses or treacle, heavy syrup obtained from grapes).

Helva

This sweet is a flaky confection of crushed sesame seeds in a base of syrup.

Maraş Dondurması

This is a special ice cream unique to Turkey. It was named after the southeastern city of *Maraş*. It is thickened and enriched with "salep" which is obtained from the root of the wild orchid and ground. This ice cream is beaten with a paddle. You can cut it with a knife.

Pişmaniye

Helva

Kestane Şekeri
(Candied Chestnuts)

TURKISH DRINKS

Turkish Coffee

Coffee-beans used to be roasted on the hearth, left to cool in a wooden bowl, ground in a brass coffee mill, and with the fresh aroma of coffee, poured into the coffee jar. The process continued by making coffee in a little brass pot with a long handle on the brazier or a spirit stove, and finally drunk from a small porcelain cup.

According to a Turkish proverb "A cup of coffee guarantees 40 years of friendship" as you can never forget a sincere and hospitable offer of a cup of bitter Turkish coffee.

Turkish coffee is a ritual rather than a drink. Although coffee is not grown in Turkey, Turks introduced it to the western world during the *Siege of Vienna* in the 16C.

It is made by mixing an extremely finely ground coffee with water and sugar. According to your taste, you should let the waiter know in advance how much sugar you like: *sade* (without sugar), *az şekerli* (a little sugar), *orta* (medium sugar) or *şekerli* (with a lot of sugar).

As the coffee begins to heat, it begins to foam. The more foam you have on the surface of the coffeecup, the more appreciation you will acquire.

Çay-Tea

The major hot drink at breakfasts, after
or in-between meals, in social gatherings
or formal business meetings is always tea.
Turks have one of the highest consumption
rates of tea in the world. Tea is widely grown
in Turkey, along the Eastern Black Sea coast.

Teahouses or tea gardens are abundant and
everywhere. Turkish people mostly
use loose tea and make tea by
using two pots, one on top of
the other. The upper one is
smaller. The lower one is for
boiling water and the top one
is for steeping the loose tea with
less water. While serving the tea in the
small tulip-shaped traditional glasses, you
will mix the two according to your taste. If you like it
strong, you will add more from the top pot.

Boza

It is a fermented and sweetened drink made from
corn or wheat.

Salep

Salep is boiled milk flavored with orchis plant. Found only in
cold winter months.

Ayran

Similar to buttermilk, this is a refreshing tangy drink of yogurt,
water and salt whipped together. It is served cold, and it's a
very common health drink. Some forms of fresh ayran come
with foam.

Wines of Turkey*

Turkey is one of the oldest lands for cultivating the grapevine for wine. The history of wine production in Anatolia dates back to 4500 years ago, to the *Bronze Age*. The *Hittites* were the first people to make laws and regulations about viticulture and wine making. The *Euphrates* and *Tigris Rivers* were used to carry wines of Eastern Turkey to the *Assyrian* and *Sumerian* lands.

In the tumulus type grave of *King Midas* of the *Phrygians* who ruled in 8C BC, the remains of wine and bread were discovered.

The biggest temples dedicated to *Dionysus*, God of wine, were in the Aegean Region of Turkey.

Turkey is the fourth largest producer of grapes in the world; however, the majority of these grapes are used to eat and in producing raisins instead of producing wine. Only 2% is used for wine.

Turkey is divided into 5 regions for wine production.

The brands listed are among the recommended wines and have been chosen from those most readily available in İstanbul.

* This section has been prepared by wine specialist Murat Yankı.

A – Average
AA – Above Average
AAA – Much Above Average

❶ *Marmara* Region (Around the *Marmara* Sea)

Local red grapes: *Papazkarası* and *Adakarası*
International red grapes: Cabernet Sauvignon,
Merlot and Gamay

Local white grapes: *Vasilaki* and *Çavuş*
International white grapes: Semillon

Recommended Wines:

Red: Sarafin Merlot (AAA), Doluca Antik (AA),
DLC Cabernet Sauvignon-Merlot (AA) and
Kavaklıdere Angora (A)

White: Sarafin Chardonnay (AAA),
Doluca Antik (AA) and Villa Doluca (A)

❷ Aegean Region (Western Anatolia)

Local red grapes: Cabernet Sauvignon, Carignan and Syrah

Local white grapes: *Misket* and *Sultaniye*
International white grapes: Chardonnay

Recommended Wines:

Red: Sevilen Syrah (AA), Sevilen Majestik (A)
and DLC Syrah (AA)

White: Kavaklıdere Angora (A), Doluca DLC Sultaniye-Emir (AA)
and Sevilen Chardonnay (AA)

Rose: Sevilen R. (A)

❸ *Pamukkale* Region (Inner Aegean)

Local red grapes: *Çalkarası*
International red grapes: Cabernet Sauvignon and Merlot

International white grapes: Chardonnay and
                                        Sauvignon Blanc

Recommended Wines:
Red: Anfora Cabernet Sauvignon (AA), Anfora Syrah (AA)

White: Anfora Senfoni (A), Anfora Chardonnay (A)

Rose: Kavaklıdere Lal (A)

❹ Central Anatolia (*Ankara*, Cappadocia and *Tokat*)

Local red grapes: *Kalecik Karası*
International red grapes: Cabernet Sauvignon and Merlot

Local white grapes: *Emir* (from *Cappadocia*),
                                 Narince (from *Tokat*)

Recommended Wines:
Red: Kavaklıdere Ancyra (AA), DLC Kalecik Karası (AA)

White: Doluca Nevşah (A), Kavaklıdere Çankaya (A),
          Kavaklıdere Narince (AAA)

❺ Eastern Turkey (Euphrates and Tigris Rivers in North Mesopotamia)

Although there is no white wine production in this region, the red wines are among the best-bodied wines of Turkey.

Local red grapes: *Boğazkere*, *Öküzgözü*

Recommended Wines:
Red: Terra Öküzgözü-Boğazkere (AA),
          Kavaklıdere Yakut (A), Doluca Kav (AA)

Rakı

Also called "lion's milk" Rakı is the national drink; a 90-proof aniseed-flavored alcohol. To drink rakı properly, one needs two long and narrow glasses. One of the glasses changes its color from a clear liquid to a milky-white when it is filled with half rakı and half water.

The other is for just plain water. The etiquette is to keep the levels of the two glasses more or less the same as you continue drinking. Rakı is generally a drink that goes with a good meal. It is drunk cold, mostly with ice and requires some sort of food, the best accompaniment being some meze. The average number of glasses for one person is between 2 and 4.

Beer

It is believed that the first beer in Anatolia was brewed at the time of the Hittites, some 3500 years ago.

The largest producer of beer in Turkey is the *Efes Beverage Group* with approximately 80% of the market share. Their main product line is called **Efes Pilsen**. The name **Efes** is the modern version of the name of the ancient city of *Ephesus*, as the brewery is close to *Ephesus*. The beer is described as having a "tangy malt and hops aroma, rich malt in the mouth, and a bitter-sweet finish that becomes dry and hoppy".

In addition to **Efes Pilsen**, Efes Beverage Group brews **Efes Light, Efes Dark, Efes Extra, Efes Ice, Marmara Kırmızı** (Red), **Marmara Gold**, **Ritmix** and **Gusta**. **Gusta** is a new product and announced to be the first beer of Turkey made of wheat. They brew *Becks, Miller, Warstiener* and *Fosters* under license.

Tuborg is also brewed in Turkey under license. *Heineken* is imported.

Drinking Water

Although water is considered safe to drink in most places in Turkey, chlorination and the different mineral contents of the tap water, particularly in the large cities such as İstanbul, can sometimes cause problems for the visitor. It is therefore advisable to drink bottled water or mineral water as a safeguard.

Even local people in İstanbul do not drink water from the tap. In fact, there are drinking water stations similar in organization to gas stations, where the locals go to "fill up" their water storage containers or buy them in large bottles that are delivered to their homes.

SELECTED RESTAURANTS

$ – Average
$$ – Above Average
$$$ – Much Above Average

• *International Cuisine Restaurants*

Flamm ($$)
Sofyalı Sk. No: 16/1
Asmalımescit, Beyoğlu
212 - 2 45 7604 - 05
www.flammist.com

Sardunya ($$)
Deniz Ticaret Odası Binası
Fındıklı
212 - 249 1092
www.sardunya.com

Sunset Grill & Bar ($$$)
Adnan Saygun Cad.
Yol Sk. No: 2, Ulus
212 - 287 0357
www.sunsetgrillbar.com

Ulus 29 ($$$)
Adnan Saygun Cad.
Yol Sk. No: 1, Ulus
212 - 358 2929
www.club29.com

360 İstanbul ($$)
İstiklal Cad. Mısır Apt.
No: 31, Beyoğlu
212 - 251 1042-43
www.360istanbul.com

Vogue ($$$)
Spor Cad. BJK Plaza
No: 92, A Blok
Akaretler, Beşiktaş
212 - 22725 45
www.istanbuldoors.com

• *Turkish Cuisine Restaurants*

Asitane ($$)
Kariye Oteli
Edirnekapı
212 - 635 7997
www.kariyeotel.com

Boğaziçi Borsa ($$)
Lütfi Kırdar Kongre Merkezi
Harbiye
212 - 232 4200
www.borsarestaurants.com

Çiya ($; no alcohol)
Güneşli Bahçe Sk. No: 43
Kadıköy
216 - 330 3190
www.ciya.com.tr

Divan ($$)
Divan Oteli
Elmadağ
212 - 315 5500
www.divan.com.tr

Feriye ($$$)
Çırağan Cad. No: 124
Beşiktaş
212 - 227 2216
www.feriye.com

Hacı Abdullah
($$; no alcohol)
Sakızağacı Cad. No: 17
Beyoğlu
212 - 293 8561
www.haciabdullah.com.tr

Hacı Baba ($$)
İstiklal Cad. No: 49
Beyoğlu
212 - 244 1886
www.hacibabarest.com

Havuzlu Restaurant ($)
Gazi Çelebi Sk. No: 3
Kapalıçarşı, Bayezit
212 - 527 3346

Hünkar ($$)
Nispetiye Cad. No: 52, Etiler
212 - 287 8470 - 71

Mim Kemal Öke Cad. No: 21
Nişantaşı
212 – 296 3811

Kanaat ($; no alcohol)
Selman İpek Cad.
Sahilyolu Sk. No: 33/A
Üsküdar

216 - 553 3792
www.kanaatlokantasi.com.tr

Konyalı ($$$)
Kanyon Alışveriş Merkezi
Levent
212 - 353 0450
www.konyalilokantasi.com

Sarnıç ($$)
Soğukçeşme Sk.
Sultanahmet
212 - 512 4291
www.turing.org.tr

Tuğra ($$$)
Çırağan Palace Kempinski
Çırağan Cad. No: 32
Beşiktaş
212 - 259 0394
www.kempinski_istanbul.com

Yanyalı Fehmi
($; no alcohol)
Söğutlüçeşme Cad.
Yağlıkçı İsmail Sk. No: 1
Kadıköy
216 - 336 3333
www.fehmilokantasi.com

Yeşil Ev ($$)
Kabasakal Cad. No: 5
Sultanahmet
212 - 517 6785
www.istanbulyesilev.com

• Meat and Kebap Restaurants

Beyti ($$)
Orman Sk. No: 8, Florya
212 - 663 2990 - 92
www.beyti.com

Develi ($$)
Balık Pazarı, Gümüşyüzük Sk.
No: 7, Samatya
212 - 529 0833
-Etiler, 212 - 263 2571
www.develikebap.com

Günaydın Et ($$)
Kasaplar Çarşısı No: 10
-Bostancı, 216 - 417 9209
Bağdat Cad. No:493/1
-Suadiye, 216 - 445 6338
Atatürk Cad. No:64
-Sahrayıcedid, 216 - 411 6875
www.gunaydinet.com

Hamdi ($$)
Tahmis Cad. Kalçın Sk. No: 17
Eminönü, 212 -528 0390
www.hamdirestaurant.com.tr

Komşu Kebap ($$)
Valikonağı Cad. Işık Apt.
No: 8/B, Nişantaşı
212 - 224 9666
www.komsukebap.com

Köşebaşı ($$)
Çamlık Sk. No:15
3. Levent
212 - 270 2433
www.kosebasi.com

Musa Usta ($)
İstiklal Cad.
Küçükparmakkapı Sk.
Beyoğlu
212 - 245 2932
www.musaustam.com

Sultanahmet Köftesi ($)
Divanyolu Cad. No: 12
Sultanahmet
212 - 520 0566
www.sultanahmetkoftesi.com

Tike ($$)
Hacı Adil Cad. 4. Aralık
2. Levent
212 - 281 8871
www.tike.com.tr

• Fish Restaurants

Balıkçı Sabahattin ($$)
Seyit Hasan Kuyu Sk. No: 1
Cankurtaran
212 - 458 1824
www.balikcisabahattin.com

Bebek Balıkçısı ($$$)
Cevdet Paşa Cad.
No: 26/A, Bebek
212 - 263 34 47
www.bebekbalikci.com

Del Mare
Ristorante ($$$)
Kuleli Cad. No:53
Çengelköy
216 - 422 5762
www.del-mare.com

Dicle Balıkevi ($)
Caferağa Mah.
Muvakkithane Cad. No: 57
Kadıköy
216 - 450 2750
www.diclebalik.com

Divan Kalamış ($$)
Amiral Fahri Korutürk
Yat Limanı, Kalamış
216 - 414 5703
www.divan.com.tr

Hanedan ($$)
Barbaros Meydanı
Çiğdem Sk. No: 27
Beşiktaş
212 - 259 0809
www.hanedanrestaurant.com

İsmet Baba ($)
İskele Yanı Çarşı Cad.
No: 96/98
Kuzguncuk
216 - 553 1232
www.ismetbaba.com.tr

Körfez Restaurant ($$$)
Körfez Cad. No: 78
Kanlıca
216 - 413 43 14
www.korfez.com

Mavi Balık ($$)
Muallim Naci Cad.
No: 64/2, Kuruçeşme
212 - 265 5480
www.mavibalik.com

Park Fora ($$$)
Muallim Naci Cad.
No: 134, Kuruçeş me
212 - 265 5067
www.parkfora.com

Poseidon ($$$)
Cevdet Paşa Cad. No: 58
Küçükbebek
212 - 263 3823
www.poseidonbistro.com

Set Balık ($)
Kireçburnu Cad.
No: 18, Tarabya
212 - 262 0411

• Meyhane

Cumhuriyet ($$)
Sahne Sk. No: 47
Beyoğlu
212 - 243 6406
www.tarihicumhuriyetmeyhanesi.com

Çiçek Pasajı ($)
İstiklal Cad. No: 172
Beyoğlu
212 - 244 2867 – 251 3680
www.tarihicicekpasaji.com

Degüstasyon ($)
Sahne Sk. No: 41
Beyoğlu
212 - 292 0667

Hatay ($)
Bağdat Cad. No: 526
Bostancı
216 - 361 3357
www.hatayrestaurant.com

İmroz ($)
Nevizade Sk. No: 24
Beyoğlu
212 - 249 9073
www.nevizadeimroz.com.tr

Kör Agop ($)
Ördekli Bakkal Sk.
No: 7, Kumkapı
212 - 517 2334
www.koragop.com

Kuleli ($)
Kuleli Sk. No: 40
Samatya
212 - 587 9428
www.kulelimeyhane.net

Refik ($)
Asmalımescit Cad.
Sofyalı Sk. No: 10/1
Tünel, Beyoğlu
212 - 243 2834
www.refikrestaurant.com

Şarabi ($)
İstiklal Cad. No: 124
Beyoğlu
212 - 244 4609
www.sarabi.com.tr

• Vegetarian Restaurants

Figaro's Restaurant ($$)
İskele Cad. Cümbüş Sk.
No: 4, Yeşilköy
212 - 662 2931
www.figarosrestaurant.com

Nature and Peace ($)
İstiklal Cad.
Büyükparmakkapı Sk.
No: 21-22, Beyoğlu
212 - 252 8609
www.natureandpeace.com

Parsifal ($)
Şehit Muhtar Mah.
Kurabiye Sk. No: 13/1
Beyoğlu
212 - 245 2588
www.parsifalde.com

Saf ($$)
Club Sporium
(Mayadrom Arkası)
Cumhuriyet Cad. No: 4/8
Akatlar
212 - 282 7946
- Tramway Yolu No: 48
(Sahil yolu - Galatasaray
Adası karşısı)
Kuruçeşme
212 - 257 0067
- Meşrutiyet Cad. No: 70
Tepebaşı, Tünel
212 - 245 88 08
www.safrestaurant.com.tr

Zencefil ($)
Kurabiye Sk. No: 8/10
Beyoğlu
212 - 243 8233 - 34

• *Pide Restaurants*

Bafra Pidecisi ($)
Hasan Amir Sk. No: 21
Kızıltoprak
216 - 336 9759
www.bafrapide.com

Fatih Karadeniz Pidecisi ($)
Büyük Karaman Cad.
No: 57, Fatih
212 - 523 9795
www.fatihkaradenizpidesi.com

Köyüm Pide ($)
Moda Cad. No: 256
Kadıköy
216 - 345 0909
www.koyumpide.com

Nizam Pide ($)
Kalyoncu Kulluk Cad.
No: 13, Beyoğlu
212 - 249 5501
www.nizampide.com

Pide ($)
Maçka Cad. No: 16/20
Teşvikiye
212 - 224 0184

• Börek Restaurants

Aslı Börek ($)
İstasyon Cad. No: 110
Göztepe
216 - 386 3534
www.asliborek.com

Sacide ($)
Bağdat Cad. No: 454
Suadiye
216 - 416 4629

Saray ($)
Teşvikiye Cad. No: 105
Teşvikiye
212 - 236 1617
www.saraymuhallebicisi.com

Tarihi Kireçburnu Fırını ($)
Kireçburnu Cad. No: 21
Sarıyer
212 - 262 1059

Tarihi Sarıyer Börekçisi ($)
Yenimahalle Cad. No: 50
Sarıyer
212 - 242 1539
www.tarihisariyerborekcisi.com

• Mantı Restaurants

Aşkana Ulus ($)
Metehan Sk. Türkel Apt.
İkinci Ulus
212 - 281 9862 – 268 7442

Casita Mantı ($)
Nispetiye Cad. No: 5, Etiler
212 - 263 7007

Emek Mantı ($)
Köybaşı Cad. No: 218
Yeniköy
212 - 262 6981
www.emekmanti.net

Fıccın Lokantası ($)
İstiklal Cad. Kallavi Sk. No: 13
Beyoğlu
212 - 293 3786
www.ficcin.com

Mantıcı ($)
Ergenekon Cad.
Tayyareci Fehmi Bey Sk.
No: 10, Pangaltı
212 - 232 3276

• Tatlıcı (Desserts, Sweets & Cakes)

Baylan ($)
Muvakkithane Cad.
No: 19, Kadıköy
216 - 346 6350
www.baylanpastanesi.com

Beyaz Fırın ($)
Cemil Topuzlu Cad. No: 21
Çiftehavuzlar
216 - 302 2428
www.beyazfirin.com

Güllüoğlu ($)
Rıhtım Cad. Kat Otoparkı Altı
Karaköy
212 - 249 9680
www.gulluoglu.biz

İnci Pastanesi ($)
İstiklal Cad. No: 124/2
Beyoğlu
212 - 243 2412

Özsüt ($)
İstiklal Cad. No: 15
Beyoğlu
212 - 293 7861
www.ozsut.com.tr

Pelit ($)
Küçük Bebek Cad. No: 3
Bebek
212 - 265 3056
www.pelit.com.tr

Saray ($)
İstiklal Cad. No: 102-104
Beyoğlu
212 - 292 3434
www.saraymuhallebicisi.com

Sarıyer Muhallebicisi ($)
Sarıyer Sahili
212 - 242 6883

Sütiş ($)
İstiklal Cad. No: 7
Beyoğlu
212 - 251 3205
www.sutis.com.tr

Zeynel ($)
Köybaşı Cad. No: 144
Yeniköy
212 - 262 8987
www.zeynel.com.tr

Next page: 5 o'clock tea at the Gazebo, Çırağan Palace Kempinski Hotel >>

Aşşk Cafe ($$)
Muallim Naci Cad. No: 64/B
Kuruçeşme
212 - 265 4734
www.asskcafe.com

Bebek Kahvesi ($)
Cevdet Paşa Cad. No: 137
Bebek
212 - 257 5402

Bebek Koru Kahvesi ($)
Cevdet Paşa Cad. No: 121
Bebek
212 - 287 5607

Cafe Creme ($)
Değirmen Sk. No: 12
Ortaköy
212 - 227 7294
www.cafecremeistanbul.com

Cafe Marmara ($$)
The Marmara Hotel
Taksim
212 - 251 4696
www.themarmarahotels.com

Carpe Diem ($$)
Bağdat Cad. No: 418
Suadiye
216 - 463 0099
www.carpediem.com.tr

Chocolate ($$)
Eytam Cad. No: 33, Maçka
212 - 343 2461
www.chocolatecafe.com.tr

Divan Pastanesi ($$)
Cevdet Paşa Cad. No: 121
Bebek
212 - 257 7270
www.divan.com.tr

Gezi İstanbul ($$)
İnönü Cad. No: 5
Taksim
212 - 292 5353
www.geziistanbul.com

İstanbul Modern Cafe ($$$)
Meclisi Mebusan Cad.
Antrepo No: 4, Karaköy
212 - 292 2612
www.istanbulmodern.org

Limonlu Bahçe ($)
Yeniçarşı Sk. No: 98
Galatasaray
212 - 252 1094

Lucca ($$$)
Cevdet Paşa Cad.
No:51/A, Bebek
212 - 257 1255
www.luccastyle.com

Passion ($$)
Valikonağı Cad. No: 111
Nişantaşı
212 - 224 8400

SELECTED HOTELS

TUROB

TUROB is a professional organization for hotel owners and managers. Most of the 4 and 5 star hotels in İstanbul are members of TUROB.

Activities of TUROB:
a) The publication of circulars and press bulletins regarding any aspect of hotel business in general;

b) The organization of monthly luncheon meetings for the purpose of encouraging solidarity among members;

c) The providing of information to members about regulations in tourism.

TUROB
Cumhuriyet Cad. Pak Apt.
Kat: 6 D: 12 (Divan Oteli Yanı)
Harbiye - Şişli
212 - 296 0880
www.turob.org

• 5-Star Hotels

Akgün Hotel İstanbul (★★★★★)
Adnan Menderes Bulvarı, Topkapı
212 - 534 4879
www.akgunhotel.com

Barcelo Eresin Topkapı (★★★★★)
Millet Cad. No: 186, Topkapı
212 - 631 1212
www.barcelo.com

By O Tell & By O Med (★★★★★)
Saniye Ermutlu Sok. No: 3
Kozyatağı
216 – 571 6100
www.byotell.com.tr

Ceylan InterContinental İstanbul (★★★★★)
Asker Ocağı Cad. , No: 1, Taksim
212   368 4444
istanbul.intercontinental.com.tr

Conrad İstanbul (★★★★★)
Yıldız Cad. Beşiktaş
212 – 227 3000
www.conradistanbul.com

Crowne Plaza İstanbul Old City (★★★★★)
Ordu Cad. Laleli
212 – 444 9333
www.crowneplaza.com

Crowne Plaza İstanbul (★★★★★)
Sahilyolu, Ataköy
212 - 560 8100
www.crowneplaza.com/istanbul

Çınar Hotel (★★★★★)
Şevketiye Mah. Fener Mevkii
Yeşilköy
212 - 663 2900
www.cinarhotel.com.tr

Çırağan Palace Kempinski (*****)
Çırağan Cad. No: 32, Beşiktaş
212 - 326 4646
www.kempinski-istanbul.com

Dedeman İstanbul (*****)
Yıldız Posta Cad. No: 50
Esentepe
212 - 337 4500
www.dedemanhotels.com

Divan İstanbul Hotel (*****)
Cumhuriyet Cad. , No: 2, Şişli
212 - 315 5500
www.divanhotels.com

Eser Premium Hotel & SPA Büyükçekmece (*****)
Gazi Mustafa Kemal Cad.
No: 11, Büyükçekmece
212 – 867 7000
www.eserhotel.com.tr

Four Seasons at the Bosphorus (*****)
Çırağan Cad. No: 28, Beşiktaş
212 – 381 4000
www.fourseasons.com

Grand Cevahir Hotel (*****)
Darülaceze Cad. No: 9 Şişli
212 – 314 4242
www.gch.com.tr

Hilton İstanbul (*****)
Cumhuriyet Cad., Harbiye
212 - 315 6000
www.istanbul.hilton.com

Holiday Inn İstanbul Airport Hotel (*****)
Taşocağı Yolu Cad. No: 35,
Bağcılar
212 – 465 8165
www.hiistanbul-airportnorth.com

Holiday Inn İstanbul City (*****)
Turgut Özal Cad. (Millet Cad.)
No:189, Topkapı
212 – 530 9900
www.hiistanbulcity.com

Hyatt Regency İstanbul (*****)
Taşkışla Cad. No: 1, Taksim
212 - 368 1234
www.istanbul.regency.hyatt.com

İstanbul Marriott Asia Hotel (*****)
Kayışdağı Cad. No: 1, Kozyatağı
216 – 570 0000
www.marriott.com

Kaya Ramada Plaza İstanbul (*****)
E5 Otoyolu Tüyap Yanı,
Büyükçekmece
212 - 886 2323
www.kayaramada.com

Kumburgaz Marin Princess Hotel (*****)
E5 Karayolu Üzeri, Kumburgaz
212 - 885 9000
www.marinprincesshotel.com

Klassis Resort Hotel (*****)
Kargaburun Mevkii, Silivri
212 - 727 4050
www.klassis.com.tr

Legacy Ottoman Hotel (*****)
Hobyar Mah. Hamidiye Cad.
No: 64, Eminönü
212 – 527 6767
www.legacyottoman.com

**Mövenpick Hotel İstanbul
(*****)**
Büyükdere Cad. 4. Levent
212 - 319 2929
www.moevenpick-istanbul.com

Ortaköy Princess (*****)
Dereboyu Cad. No: 36-38,
Ortaköy
212 – 227 6010
www.ortakoyprincess.com

**Polat Renaissance İstanbul
Hotel (*****)**
Sahil Cad. No: 2, Yeşilyurt
212 - 414 1800
www.polatrenaissance.com

**Radisson Sas Bosphorus Hotel
(*****)**
Çırağan Cad. No: 46, Ortaköy
212 – 260 5757
www.istanbul.radissonsas.com

**Radisson Sas
Conference&Airport (*****)**
E5 Karayolu Üzeri, Sefaköy
212 - 425 7373
www.istanbul.airport.radissonsas.com

Ramada Plaza İstanbul (*****)
Halaskargazi Cad. No: 63,
Osmanbey
212 – 315 4444
www.ramadaplazaistanbul.com

**Sheraton İstanbul Ataköy
(*****)**
Sahilyolu Ataköy
212 – 560 8100
www.sheratonistanbulatakoy.com.tr

**Sheraton İstanbul Maslak
(*****)**
Büyükdere Cad. No: 233
212 – 335 9999
www.sheratonistanbulmaslak.com

**Swissotel The Bosphorus
İstanbul (*****)**
Bayıldım Cad. No: 2, Maçka
212 - 326 1100
www.swissotel.com

Sürmeli İstanbul Hotel (*****)
Prof. Dr. Bülent Tarcan Sk.
No: 3, Gayrettepe
212 – 272 1161
www.surmelihotels.com

The Marmara İstanbul (*****)
Taksim Meydanı, Taksim
212 - 251 4696
www.themarmarahotels.com

**The Plaza Hotel İstanbul
(*****)**
Barbaros Bulvarı No: 165
Balmumcu, Beşiktaş
212 – 370 2020
www.theplazahotel.com.tr

**The Ritz-Carlton, İstanbul
(*****)**
Süzer Plaza, Elmadağ
212 - 334 4444
www.ritzcarlton.com.tr

WOW İstanbul Hotel (*****)
Dünya Ticaret Merkezi, Yeşilköy
212 – 468 5000
www.wowhotelistanbul.com

• 4-Star Hotels

Airport Güneş Hotel (****)
Nadide Cad. Günay Sk.
No: 1, Merter
212 – 483 3030
www.guneshotel.com.tr

Antik Hotel (****)
Ordu Cad. Sekbanbaşı Sk.
No: 10, Beyazıt
212 - 638 5858
www.antikhotel.com

Arcadia Hotel İstanbul (****)
Dr. İmran Öktem Sk. No: 1
Sultanahmet
212 - 516 9696
www.hotelarcadiaistanbul.com

Armada Hotel İstanbul (****)
Ahırkapı Cad. No: 24, Ahırkapı
212 – 455 4480
www.armadahotel.com.tr

Ata Hotel (****)
Merkez Mah. Menekşe Sk.
Umut Cad. No: 1, Kumburgaz
212 – 885 3848
www.atahotel.com.tr

Ataköy Marina İstanbul (****)
Sahilyolu Ataköy
212 – 560 4110
www.atakoymarinahotel.com.tr

Aziyade Hotel (****)
Piyerloti Cad. No: 62,
Sultanahmet
212 – 638 2200
www.aziyadehotel.com

Best Western Eresin Taxim Hotel (****)
Topçu Cad. No: 34, Taksim
212 - 256 0803
www.eresintaxim.com.tr

Best Western Senator Hotel (****)
Gençtürk Cad. Şirvanizade Sk.
No: 7/11, Şehzadebaşı
212 - 528 1865
www.senatorhotel.com

Best Western The President Hotel (****)
Tiyatro Cad. No: 25, Beyazıt
212 - 516 6980
www.thepresidenthotel.com

Black Bird Hotel (****)
Gençtürk Cad. No: 51/53
Şehzadebaşı
212 - 511 7454
www.blackbirdhotel.com

Büyük Şahinler Hotel (****)
Mesihpaşa Cad. No: 73, Laleli
212 - 518 7440
www.hotelbuyuksahinler.com

Çara Hotel İstanbul (****)
Koca Ragıppaşa Cad.
No: 19, Laleli
212 - 638 8900
www.carahotel.com.tr

Courtyard by Marriott (****)
Fatih Cad. Dereboyu Sk.
No: 6/A, Halkalı
212 – 698 5243
www.courtyard.com/istcy

Crystal Hotel İstanbul(****)
Receppaşa Cad. No: 9, Taksim
212 – 237 8500
www.crystalhotel.net

Dilson Hotel (****)
Sıraselviler Cad. No: 49, Taksim
212 - 252 9600
www.dilson.com

Divan City İstanbul (****)
Büyükdere Cad. No: 84,
Gayrettepe
212 – 337 4900
www.divan.com.tr

**Dream Hill Business
Deluxe Hotel (****)**
Bağdat Cad. No: 273, Maltepe
216 – 458 0000
www.dreamhillhotel.com

Elite Hotel (****)
Kocatepe Mah. Şehit Muhtar
Cad. No: 40, Taksim
212 - 297 1313
www.elitehotel.com.tr

**Eresin Taxim &
Premier Hotel (****)**
Topçu Cad. No: 16, Taksim
212 – 256 0803
www.eresintaxim.com.tr

Feronya Hotel (****)
Abdülhakhamit Cad.
No: 58, Taksim
212 – 238 0866
www.feronya.com

Golden Age 1 (****)
Topçu Cad. No: 22, Taksim
212 - 254 4906
www.goldenagehotel.com

Golden Park Hotel (****)
Lamartin Cad. No: 24, Taksim
212 – 361 4141
www.hotelgoldenpark.net

Grand Anka Hotel (****)
Molla Gürani Cad. No: 46,
Fındıkzade
212 - 635 2020
www.grandankahotel.com

Grand Öztanık (****)
Topçu Cad. No: 9-11, Taksim
212 – 361 6080
www.grandoztanik.com.tr

Grand Star Hotel (****)
Sıraselviler Cad. No: 79, Taksim
212 - 252 7070
www.hotelgrandstar.com.tr

Grand Yavuz Hotel (****)
Pier Loti Cad. No: 71/B,
Sultanahmet
212 – 517 1712
www.grandyavuzhotel.com

Güneş Hotel (****)
Nadide Cad. Günay Sk.
No: 10, Merter
212 - 483 3030
www.guneshotel.com.tr

Hilton Parksa (****)
Bayıldım Cad. No: 12, Maçka
212 - 310 1200
www.istanbul-park.hilton.com

Holiday Inn İstanbul (****)
Sahilyolu, Ataköy
212 - 560 4110
www.holiday-inn.com/
atakoymarina

Hotel İstanbul Conti (****)
Ortaklar Cad. No: 30,
Mecidiyeköy
212 - 288 1642
www.istanbulconti.com.tr

**Hotel İstanbul Kervansaray
(****)**
Şehit Muhtar Cad.
No: 61, Taksim
212 - 235 5000
www.kervansarayistanbul.com

Hotel Yaşmak Sultan (****)
Ebusuud Cad. No: 18/20, Sirkeci
212 - 528 1343
www.hotelyasmaksultan.com

Hotel Yenişehir Palas (****)
Meşrutiyet Cad. Oteller Sk.
No: 1/3, Tepebaşı
212 - 252 7160
www.yenisehirpalas.com

Hotel Yiğitalp (****)
Gençtürk Cad. Çukurçeşme Sk.
No: 38, Şehzadebaşı
212 - 512 9860
www.yigitalp.com

İstanbul Royal Hotel (****)
Aksaray Cad. No: 16, Laleli
212 - 518 5151
www.istanbulroyalhotel.com

Kalyon Hotel (****)
Sahilyolu Sultanahmet
212 – 517 4400
www.kalyon.com

Kent Hotel İstanbul (****)
Haznedar Sok. No: 2-4, Beyazıt
212 – 638 2985
www.istanbulkenthotel.com

Konak Hotel (****)
Cumhuriyet Cad. No: 75,
Elmadağ
212 - 225 8250
www.konakhotel.com

Lady Diana Hotel (****)
Binbirdirek Mah. Terzihane Sk.
No: 9, Sultanahmet
212 – 516 9642
www.ladydianahotel.com

Larespark Hotel Taksim İstanbul (****)
Topçu Cad. No: 23, Taksim
212 – 313 5100
www.laresparkhotel.com

Lion Hotel İstanbul (****)
Lamartin Cad. No: 45, Taksim
212 – 256 9090
www.lionhotel.net

Marble Hotel (****)
Sıraselviler Cad. No: 41, Taksim
212 - 252 6344 – 252 3597
www.marblehotel.com

Midtown Hotel İstanbul (****)
Lamartin Cad. No: 13, Taksim
212 – 361 6767
www.midtown-hotel.com

Novotel İstanbul (****)
Kazlıçeşme Mah. Kennedy Cad.
No: 56, Zeytinburnu
212 – 414 3600
www.novotel.com

Orsep Royal Hotel (****)
Hocapaşa Mah. Nöbethane Cad.
No: 10, Sirkeci
212 – 511 8585
www.orseproyalhotel.com

Pera Tulip Hotel (****)
Meşrutiyet Cad. No: 103,
Beyoğlu
212 – 243 8500
www.peratulip.com

Point Hotel (****)
Topçu Cad. No: 8, Taksim
212 – 313 5000
www.pointhotel.com

Prince Hotel (****)
Nöbethane Cad. Kargılı Sk.
No: 5, Sirkeci
212 - 513 2550
www.hotelprince.com

Ramada Old City Hotel(****)
Millet Cad. No: 82, Fındıkzade
212 – 631 2020
www.colorhotel.com

Richmond İstanbul (****)
Istiklal Cad. No: 227, Tünel
212 - 252 5460
www.richmondhotels.com.tr

The Green Park Hotel Taksim (****)
Abdülhakhamit Cad.
No: 50, Taksim
212 – 444 7275
www.thegreenpark.com

The Madison Hotel (****)
Receppaşa Cad. No: 15, Taksim
212 - 238 5460
www.madison.com.tr

The Marmara Pera (****)
Meşrutiyet Cad. Tepebaşı
212 - 251 4646
www.themarmarahotels.com

The Marmara Şişli (****)
Ortaklar Cad. No: 30,
Mecidiyeköy
212 – 370 9400
www.themarmarahotels.com

The Peak Hotel (****)
Meşrutiyet Cad. Oteller Sk.
No: 1/3, Tepebaşı, Beyoğlu
212 – 252 7160
www.thepeakhotel.com.tr

Topkapı İnter İstanbul Hotel (****)
Topkapı Cad. No: 8
Kaleiçi, Topkapı
212 – 491 2300
www.topkapiinteristanbulhotel.com

WOW Airport Hotel (****)
Dünya Ticaret Merkezi, Yeşilköy
212 – 468 3000
www.wowhotelistanbul.com

Yaşmak Sultan (****)
Ebusuud Cad. No: 18-20, Sirkeci
212- 528 1343
www.hotelyasmaksultan.com

Yiğitalp Hotel (****)
Gençtürk Cad. Çukurçeşme Sk.
No: 38, Şehzadebaşı
212 – 512 9860
www.yigitalp.com

Zurich Hotel Villa(****)
Akarsu Yokuşu Cad.
No: 44-46, Cihangir
212 - 293 0604
www.hotelvillazurich.com

Zurich Hotel (****)
Vidinli Tevfik Paşa Cad.
Harikzadeler Sk. No: 37, Laleli
212 - 512 2350
www.hotelzurichistanbul.com

• 3-Star Hotels

Barın Hotel (***)
Fevziye Cad. No: 7 Şehzadebaşı
212 – 513 9100
www.barinhotel.com

Best Western Hotel Amber (***)
Küçükayasofya Mah.
Cinci Meydanı Yusuf Aşkın Sk.
No: 28, Sultanahmet
212 - 518 4801
www.hotelamber.com

Erboy Hotel (***)
Ebusuud Cad. , No: 32, Sirkeci
212 – 513 3750
www.erboyhotel.com

Eyfel Hotel (***)
Kurultay Sk. No: 19, Laleli
212 - 520 9788 – 520 9789
www.hoteleyfel.com

Ferhat Hotel (***)
Binbirdirek Mah. Terzihane Sk.
No: 9, Sultanahmet
212 - 516 9642
www.hotelferhat.com

Golden Age 2 (***)
Abdülhakhamit Cad.
No: 60, Taksim
212 – 235 8160
www.goldenagehotel.com

Grand Ons Hotel (***)
Azimkar Sk. No: 32, Laleli
212 - 518 6370
www.grandons.com

Grand Washington (***)
Gençtürk Cad. No: 7, Laleli
212 – 511 6371
www.grand-washington.com

Green Anka Hotel (***)
Fındıkzade Sk. No: 4, Fındıkzade
212 - 631 1721
www.greenankahotel.com

Harem Hotel (***)
Selimiye Ambarı Sk.
No: 2, Üsküdar
216 - 310 6800
www.haremhotel.com

Hotel My Dora (***)
Rıhtım Cad. Recaizade Sk.
No: 6, Kadıköy
216 – 414 8350
www.hotelmydora.com

İbis Otel İstanbul (***)
Kazlıçeşme Mah. Kennedy Cad.
No: 56, Zeytinburnu
212 – 414 3900
www.ibishotel.com

Interroyal Hotel (***)
Bala Sok. No: 19, Beyoğlu
212 – 292 8230
www.interroyal.com.tr

Klassis Golf Country Club (***)
Altıntepe Mevkii Seymen Köyü,
Silivri
212 – 710 1300
www.klassis.com.tr

Taşlık Hotel (***)
Süleyman Seba Cad. No: 75
Valideçeşme, Maçka
212 - 227 8310
www.taslikhotel.com

The Grand Engin (***)
Rıhtım Cad. Tayyareci Sami Sk.
No: 17, Kadıköy
216 - 414 8350
www.hotelengin.com

Washington Hotel (★★★)
Gençtürk Ağa Yokuşu Cad. No:
12, Şehzadebaşı
212 – 520 5990
www.hotel-washington.com

• 2-Star Hotels

Avicenna Hotel (★★)
Mimar Mehmet Ağa Cad. Amiral
Tafdil Sk. No: 31-33, Sultanahmet
212 – 517 0550
www.avicennahotel.com

**Best Western Taşhan Business
& Airport Hotel (★★)**
Taşhan Cad. No: 57, Bakırköy
212 - 543 6575 – 572 8540
www.tashan.com.tr

Hotel Erdim (★★)
Ankara Cad. No: 156, Kartal
216 - 306 5894

Hotel İpek Palas (★★)
Orhaniye Cad. No: 9, Sirkeci
212 – 520 9724
www.hotelipekpalas.com

Pisa Hotel (★★)
Fethi Bey Cad. Kurultay Sk.
No: 3/1, Laleli
212 – 526 1878
www.pisahotelistanbul.com

**Sultanahmet Palace
Hotel & Restaurant (★★)**
Torun Sk. No: 19, Sultanahmet
212 - 458 0460
www.sultanahmetpalace.com

• Special Category
(Boutique) Hotels

**Acropol Hotel Best Western
(S)**
Akbıyık Cad. No: 25,
Sultanahmet
212 - 638 9021
www.acropolhotel.com

**Amiral Palace Hotel İstanbul
(S)**
Bayram Fırını Sk. Cankurtaran
Mah. No: 7, Sultanahmet
212 – 458 6800
www.amiralpalacehotel.com

Arena Hotel (S)
K. Ayasofya Mah. Üçlerhamamı
Sk. No: 13-15, Sultanahmet
212 - 458 0364
www.arenahotel.com

Barcelo Saray Hotel (S)
Yeniçeriler Cad. No: 85, Beyazıt
212   458 9800
www.barceloturkey.com

Best Western Citadel Hotel (S)
Kennedy Cad. Sahilyolu
No: 32, Ahırkapı
212 - 516 2313
www.citadelhotel.com

**Best Western Empire Palace
İstanbul (S)**
Hocapaşa Mah.
Hüdavendigar Cad.
No: 17/19, Sirkeci
212 - 514 5400
www.hotelempirepalace.com

Beyaz Saray The Hotel (S)
Yeniçeriler Cad. No: 85, Beyazıt
212 - 458 9800
www.beyazsaray.com.tr

Celal Sultan Hotel (S)
Yerebatan Cad. Salkım Söğüt Sk.
No: 16, Sultanahmet
212 – 520 9323
www.celalsultan.com

Eresin Crown De Luxe (S)
Küçük Ayasofya Cad. No: 40,
Sultanahmet
212 - 638 4428
www.eresincrown.com.tr

Four Seasons Hotel (S)
Tevkifhane Sk. No: 1,
Sultanahmet
212 - 638 8200
www.fourseasons.com

Fuat Paşa Oteli (S)
Çayırbaşı Cad. No: 148
Büyükdere, Sarıyer
212 - 242 9860
www.fuatpasa.com.tr

Germir Palas Hotel (S)
Cumhuriyet Cad. No: 17, Taksim
212 – 361 1110
www.germirpalas.com

Hotel Restaurant Hilde (S)
Büyükdere Kilyos Yolu No: 6
Bahçeköy, Sarıyer
212 - 226 1202

Hotel Uyan (S)
Utangaç Sk. No: 25, Sultanahmet
212 - 518 9255
www.uyanhotel.com

Lush Hip Hotel (S)
Sıraselviler Cad. No: 12, Taksim
212 – 243 9595
www.lushhotel.com

Masi Hotel (S)
Çakmak Mah. Mithatpaşa Cad.
Başak Sk. No: 4, Ümraniye
216 – 461 1414
www.hotelmasi.com

Mina Hotel Sultanahmet (S)
Piyerloti Cad. Dostluk Yurdu Sk.
No: 6, Sultanahmet
212 – 458 2800
www.minahotel.com.tr

Ottoman Hotel Imperial (S)
Caferiye Sok. No: 6/1,
Sultanahmet
212 – 513 6151
www.ottomanhotelimperial.com

**Park Hyatt İstanbul –
Maçka Palas (S)**
Bronz Sok. No: 4, Teşvikiye
212 – 315 1234
istanbul.park.hyatt.com

Pera Palas (S)
Meşrutiyet Cad. No: 98/100,
Tepebaşı
212 - 251 4560
www.perapalas.com

Pera Rose Hotel (S)
Meşrutiyet Cad. No: 87, Beyoğlu
212 – 243 1500
www.perarose.com

Romance Hotel (S)
Hüdavendigar Cad. No: 7, Sirkeci
212 – 512 8676
www.romancehotel.com

Ortaköy Mosque

Sultanahmet Sarayı Otel (S)
Torun Sok. No: 19, Sultanahmet
212 – 458 0460
www.sultanahmetpalace.com

The Sofa Hotel (S)
Teşvikiye Cad. No: 123, Nişantaşı
212 – 368 1818
www.thesofahotel.com

W Hotel (S)
Süleyman Seba Cad.
No: 22, Akaretler
212 – 381 2121
www.whotels.com

Vardar Palace Hotel (S)
Sıraselviler Cad. No: 16, Taksim
212 - 252 2888 – 244 5548
www.vardarhotel.com

GLOSSARY

A

ağa (Tr.)　　　　squire; village notable or landowner

Anastasis　　　　Resurrection; Christ, who has just broken down
the gates of Hell, stands in the middle and tries to
pull Adam and the Virgin Mary out of their tombs

ANZAC　　　　Australian and New Zealand Army Corps

apse　　　　a projecting part of a basilica or church building
which is semicircular and vaulted

aqueduct　　　　L aqua, water and ducere, to lead; a structure
built to carry water from a source to
a distant destination

Assumption　　　　Taking (Assuming) of the Virgin Mary bodily into
heavenly glory when she died

B

basilica　　　　a large, oblong building used particularly as a
court of law and a place of public assembly

bas-relief　　　　F bas, low + relief, raised work; sculptural relief in
which the projection from the surrounding
surface is slight and no part of the modeled
form is undercut

bedesten (Tr.)　　　　an Ottoman shopping center built with equal domes

beşik tonoz (Tr.)　　　　barrel vault

Bey (Ir.)　　　　a lord, squire

birun (Tr.)　　　　outer palace (Ottoman period)

burç (Tr.)　　　　bastion

C

caique　　　　derives from Tr. kayik; a type of small boat

Caliph　　　　Successor of the Prophet Mohammed

cami (Tr.)　　　　mosque

capital　　　　the part of a column crowning the shaft;
it originates from stone pieces put on top of
wooden columns to prevent rotting

cella naos; the inner sanctuary of a temple containing the cult statue

colonnade a series of columns set at regular intervals supporting the base of a roof structure

Composite capital a capital combining andular Ionic volutes with the acanthus-circled bell of the Corinthian

Corinthian a bell-shaped capital enveloped with acanthuses

cumba (Tr.) bay window

D

Deesis depiction of Jesus as the pantocrator flanked by the Virgin Mary and Saint John the Baptist who are shown interceding with him on behalf of mankind

defterdar (Tr.) Ottoman finance minister

dikilitaş (Tr.) obelisk

dirlik (Tr.) fief, a feudal estate

Divan (Tr.) Ottoman administration and government

Dormition falling asleep of the Virgin Mary

E

Enderun (Tr.) Ottoman Royal School; inner palace (Ottoman period)

F

ferman (Tr.) edict or decree ordered by the Sultan

forum L foris, outside; open space in any Roman city where business, judicial, municipal affairs and religious activities were conducted

G

gaza (Tr.) holy war

gazi (Tr.) fighter for the faith of Islam against the infidels

göbek taşı (Tr.) (navel stone) a marble, heated table on which people lie in a hamam

H

Hac (Tr.)   for Moslems visiting Mecca on a pilgrimage

hacı (Tr.)   Moslem pilgrim

hadis (Tr.)   recital and transmission of the words of the Prophet

han (Tr.)   caravansary; a building consisting of shops where same kind of merchandise is produced and places for people to stay

has (Tr.)   a classification of land use in the Ottoman period; see the Ottoman land administration

harem (Tr.)   private sector of a Moslem household in which women live and work

Hellenistic   of or relating to a Greek-Anatolian mixture of history, culture, or art of the period after Alexander the Great

Hicret (Tr.)   Hegira, migration of Mohammed from Mecca to Medina in 622 AD which marks the beginning of the religious calendar.

hippodrome   Gr. hipp- horse + dromos, racecourse; places for chariot races wider than the horseshoe-shaped stadiums

I

Iconoclasm   Gr. eikon, image + klan, to break; the practice of destroying religious images or opposing their veneration

Iconography   Gr. eikon, image + graphia, writing; the study of the subject matter, or content, of works of art, as opposed to their style

imam (Tr.)   prayer leader in a mosque

imaret (Tr.)   kitchens for the public, generally the poor

Islam   A islam, the act of committing oneself unreservedly to God; the religious faith of Moslems

J

janissary   *yeniceri*, a soldier of an elite corps of Ottoman troops organized in the 14th century and abolished in 1826

K

Kaaba
a shrine in Mecca that had for some time housed the idols of the pagan Meccans, was rededicated to the worship of Allah and has become the object of pilgrimage for all Moslems

kapıkulu soldier (Tr.) a class in the Ottoman army

Kaptan-ı Derya (Tr.) Commander in chief of the Ottoman fleet

kasır (Tr.)
summer palace

kathisma
royal box in a hippodrome

kazasker (Tr.)
Ottoman minister responsible for the military

kervansaray (Tr.)
Per. kervan, caravan + saray, palace; caravansary

kese (Tr.)
special gloves for rubbing the body in a hamam

kıble (Tr.)
the direction of Kaaba in Mecca faced by Moslems from all over the world during prayer

Koimesis
Dormition, falling asleep of the Virgin Mary

konak (Tr.)
mansion

Koran
Holy Book of the Moslems

köşk (Tr.)
kiosk, summer residence, pavilion

kufi (Tr.)
a formal style in calligraphy with an angular character

külliye (Tr.)
complex of buildings

kümbet (Tr.)
domed or conical-roofed tomb

L

lahit (Tr.)
sarchophagus, a stone coffin

M

mahya (Tr.)
lights stretched on special occasions between the minarets of mosques with some figures, words or expressions

mangal (Tr.)
brazier

maaşallah (Tr.)
"god preserve him"

medrese (Tr.)
Islamic theological school

mescit (Tr.)
small mosque; a place to prostrate one's self in front of God

mihrab (Tr.)   apse in a mosque

minber (Tr.)   pulpit in a mosque

minare (Tr.)   minaret, tower in a mosque from which the muezzin calls people to prayer

Moslem, Muslim   believer of Islam

müezzin (Tr.)   somebody who calls people to prayer and assists imam during prayer in a mosque

N

nalın (Tr.)   wooden clogs

namaz   act of praying or set of prayers

nargile (Tr.)   hookah, waterpipe

narthex   a narrow vestibule in a basilica or church

nazar boncuğu (Tr.)   blue eye used to ward off evil influences from others

niş (Tr.)   niche

nişancı (Tr.)   general secretary of Ottoman administration

Nizam-ı Cedit (Tr.)   late Ottoman organized army, meaning the New Order

O

omphalos   a beehive-shaped stone at Delphi, designating that spot as the center or navel of the Earth

P

pah (Tr.)   bevel, the slant or inclination of a surface

pantocrator   creator of all things and ruler of universe

paracclesion   funerary chapel

paşa (Tr.)   pasha; an army officer of high rank

Pax Romana   200 years of peace during the reign of the Roman Empire Augustus (1C BC) when the Roman Empire was at its height with no rivals.

payanda (Tr.)   buttress

pediment   triangular gable of a two-pitched roof

peştemal (Tr.)   a piece of cotton cloth worn when in a hamam

Ramazan (Tr.)	Ramadan, the 9th month of the Moslem year observed as sacred with fasting practiced daily from sunrise to sunset
revak (Tr.)	colonnade
Rum (Tr.)	Christian Greeks of Anatolia

saçak (Tr.)	eaves
sahın (Tr.)	nave (in a mosque)
sancak (Tr.)	standard, banner or flag representing the Caliphate of the Sultan
sanduka (Tr.)	coffin
saray (Tr.)	palace
sarcophagus	Gr. sarc-, flesh + phagein, to eat; flesh-eating stone (probably comes from local Assos stone), a stone coffin
savat (Tr.)	niello, the art of decorating metal with incised designs filled with niello (usually an alloy of sulfur with silver)
sema	rite of communal recitation practiced by the Mevlevis
semahane (Tr.)	hall in which sema is performed
sericulture	cultivation of silk worms for industry
Shamanism	a religion characterized by belief in an unseen world of gods, demons, and ancestral spirits responsive only to the shamans who are priests using magic
sofra (Tr.)	a tray or table on which meal is eaten
son cemaat yeri (Tr.)	outer narthex of a mosque in the courtyard for latecomers to the prayer
sorguç (Tr.)	plume
spina	barrier or the central axis of a Roman amphitheater or hippodrome

stele	an inscribed or carved upright stone slab or shaft that served as a monument, memorial, or marker
sünnet (Tr.)	whatever the prophet does or says in Islam; circumcision
synod	Church Council. A special council of church members that holds regular meetings to discuss religious issues
synthronon	semicircular rows of seats for the clergy in a church

Ş

şadırvan (Tr.)	ablution fountain
şerefe (Tr.)	minaret balcony
şeriat (Tr.)	Canonical Law (Islamic)
Şeyhülislam (Tr.)	authorized head of religious matters in Ottoman Empire

T

tekke (Tr.)	dervish monastery
tellak (Tr.)	hamam attendant who does the kese work
tımar (Tr.)	a classification of land use in the Ottoman period; see the Ottoman land administration
tuğra (Tr.)	monogram of a Sultan
tümülüs	grave formed by piles of soil
türbe (Tr.)	a domed tomb

U

ulufe (Tr.)	salary paid to Ottoman soldiers

V

vakıf (Tr.)	trust, foundation
vitray (Tr.)	stained glass

Y

yalı (Tr.)	Waterfront wooden mansion or villa on the Bosphorus
yeniçeri (Tr.)	Tr. *yeni*, new + ceri, soldier; see **janissary**

APRIL

- International İstanbul Film Festival
- International İstanbul Tulip Festival *(Second week)*
- National Independence and Children's Day *(April 23)*

MAY

- Ahırkapı Hıdrellez Festival *(Evening of May 5)*
- Formula 1 Grand Prix İstanbul *(Second weekend)*
- Atatürk Commemoration Youth and Sports Day *(May 19)*
- International İstanbul Theater Festival
  (Third week of May through the first week of June)

JUNE

- International İstanbul Music Festival
- International İstanbul Dance Festival *(First week)*
- Red Bull Air Race *(Second or third week)*
- Efes Pilsen One Love Festival *(Third weekend)*
- Open-air concerts Rumeli Fortress

JULY

- International İstanbul Jazz Festival *(First three weeks)*
- Asia to Europe International Bosphorus Swimming
  Competition *(Third weekend)*
- Open-air concerts at the Rumeli Fortress

İSTANBUL EVENTS CALENDAR

AUGUST
- Victory Day *(August 30)*
- Open-air concerts at the Rumeli Fortress

SEPTEMBER
- Rock'n Coke İstanbul *(First weekend)*
- International İstanbul Biennial
  (Third week of September through the second week of November)

OCTOBER
- İstanbul Design Week *(Second week)*
- İstanbul Eurasia Marathon *(Third or fourth Sunday)*
- Republic Day *(October 29)*

NOVEMBER
- Efes Pilsen Blues Festival
  (First week of November through the second week of December)

DECEMBER
- Contemporary İstanbul Art Festival
  (Third and fourth weeks)

BIBLIOGRAPHY

Akurgal Ekrem, *Ancient Civilizations and Ruins of Turkey*, Haşet, 1985

Akyıldız Erhan, *Taş Çağı'ndan Osmanlı'ya Anadolu*, Milliyet, 1990

Altun Ara, *Turkish Architecture in the Middle Ages*, Arkeoloji ve Sanat Yayınları, 1990

Ana Britannica, Ana Yayıncılık, 1988

Aslanapa Oktay, *Türk Sanatı*, Remzi Kitabevi, 1984

Atasoy Nurhan Dr., *Splendors of the Ottoman Sultans*, Wonders, 1992

Ayyıldız Uğur, *The Kariye Museum*, İstanbul, Net Turistik Yayınlar A.Ş., 1988

Balaman Ali Rıza, *Gelenekler Töre ve Törenler*, Betim, 1983

Belge Murat, *İstanbul Gezi Rehberi*, Tarih Vakfı, 1993

Berlitz, *The Travelers Guide to Turkey*, 1993

Boratav Pertev Naili, *100 Soruda Türk Folkloru*, Gerçek, 1984

Brosnahan Tom, *Turkey, A Survival Kit*, Lonely Planet, 1985

Buckler McKay Hill, *A History of World Societies*, Houghton Mifflin, 1988

Campbell Joseph, *Creative Mythology*, Penguin, 1968

Cornucopia in Turkey, Issue III, Volume I, 1992/93

Croutier Alev Lytle, *Harem: Peçeli Dünya*, Yılmaz Yayınları, 1990

Cumhuriyet Dönemi Türkiye Ansiklopedisi, İletişim, 1983

Çağdaş Liderler Ansiklopedisi, İletişim, 1986

Donagh Mc Bernard, *Blue Guide Turkey*, A & C Black, 1995

Dünden Bugüne İstanbul Ansiklopedisi, Tarih Vakfı, 1993, 1994

Encarta, The Complete Interactive Multimedia Encyclopedia, Microsoft, 1995

Encyclopedia Britannica, 1995

Encyclopedia of Archeology, Larousse, 1972

Encyclopedia International, Grolier, 1975

Erhat Azra, *Mitoloji Sözlüğü*, Remzi Kitabevi, 1984

Eyice Semavi Prof. Dr., *Ayasofya*, Yapı ve Kredi Bankası, 1984

Freely John, *Blue Guide İstanbul*, A & C Black, 1987

Gülersoy Çelik, *A Guide to İstanbul*, Director General of the Touring and Automobile Club of Turkey, 1978

Insight Guides, Turkey, APA Publications, 1990

İstanbul Ansiklopedisi, Türk Tarih Vakfı ve Kültür Bakanlığı, 1994

İstanbul, Turkey, Knopf Guides, 1993

İl İl Büyük Türkiye Ansiklopedisi, Milliyet

İzer Müheyya, *Baharatın İzleri*, Redhouse, 1988

Kinross Lord, *Atatürk*, The Rebirth of a Nation, Rustem, 1990

Lloyd Seton, *Ancient Turkey*, University of California Press, 1989

Necatigil Behçet, *100 Soruda Mitologya*, Gerçek, 1969

New Larousse Encyclopedia of Mythology, Hamlyn, 1978

New Perspectives on Turkey, Vassar College, 1992

Örf ve Adetlerimiz, Türk Kültürüne Hizmet Vakfı

Özcan İsmail, *İslam Ansiklopedisi*, Milliyet Yayınları, 1991

Sevin Veli, *Anadolu Arkeolojisinin ABC'si*, Simavi, 1991

Sözen Metin, Tanyeli Uğur, *Sanat Kavram ve Terimleri Sözlüğü*, Remzi, 1986

Stoneman Richard, *A Traveler's History of Turkey*, Interlink Books, 1993

Tanilli Server, *Uygarlık Tarihi*, Say, 1981

Taşlıklıoğlu Zafer, *Grekçe Gramer ve Syntaks*, Edebiyat Fakültesi Matbaası,1968

Tavernier Jean Baptiste, *Topkapı Sarayında Yaşam*, Çağdaş Yayınları, 1984

Toker Biltin, *Spot on İstanbul*, P.P.I., 1986

Tunay İ. Mehmet, *Sanat Tarihi Ders Notları*, Yeni Gün, 1977

Tuncer Ömer, *İşte Anadolu*, Arkeoloji ve Sanat Yayınları, 1993

Turkey-A Country Study, The American University, 1979

Turkey-A Phaidon Cultural Guide, Phaidon Press Limited, 1989

Turkey-A Times Bartholomew Guide, 1990

Turkey, Directorate General of Press and Information, 1993

Turkey, The Real Guide, Prentice Hall Press, 1991

Turkish Musical Instruments, Net Group of Companies, Calendar, 1995

Türkiyemiz Kültür ve Sanat Dergisi, Akbank, 1991

Türkoğlu Sabahattin, *The Topkapı Palace*, Net Turistik Yayınlar A.Ş., 1989

Unger Merrill F., *Archeology and the New Testament*, Zondervan Publishing House, 1962

Yenen Şerif, *Turkish Odyssey*, 2008

Yurtbaşı Metin, *Turkish Proverbs*, Turkish Daily News, 1993

Wycherley R.E., *Antik Çağda Kentler Nasıl Kuruldu?*, Arkeoloji ve Sanat, 1991

INDEX

371